Roy Williamson is an Ho
the Diocese of Southwell and was previously Bishop
of Bradford (1984–91) and Bishop of Southwark
(1991–98). He was also Archdeacon of Nottingham and
the incumbent of three parishes in that city. His previous
books include *Can You Spare a Minute?* and *For Such a
Time as This* (published by DLT) and *Joyful Uncertainty,
Open Return, Not Least in the Kingdom* and *Wholly
Alive* (all SPCK). He is married with three sons, two
daughters and seven grandchildren.

Loved by Love

*Growing into Spiritual Health
and Wholeness*

Roy Williamson

First published in Great Britain in 2004
Society for Promoting Christian Knowledge
Holy Trinity Church
Marylebone Road
London NW1 4DU

British Library Cataloguing-in-Publication Data
A catalogue record for this book is available from the British
Library

ISBN 0-281-05619-6

1 3 5 7 9 10 8 6 4 2

Typeset by FiSH Books, London WC1
Printed in Great Britain by Bookmarque Ltd, Croydon, Surrey

Contents

For
Roy McMullan
a friend from childhood and
a loving brother in Christ

Acknowledgements

Once again I am grateful to my editor Alison Barr for her warm encouragement and practical advice, and to Jean Cherry for reading the text and offering suggestions for improvement.

Unless otherwise stated, all biblical quotations are taken from the New Revised Standard Version.

I have altered, of course, the names and locations of the various people mentioned in order to preserve their anonymity.

Introduction

'All you need is love – love is all you need', sang the Beatles to great effect in the 'swinging sixties'. Their song was a smash hit, topping the record charts and expressing the optimism of that particular decade. And it has stood the test of time. The song is still known and loved by millions all over the world, and was chosen to be sung by children and choirs across the United Kingdom to mark the Queen's Golden Jubilee in 2002.

But is it true? Is love really all you need? Was it true in the emerging optimism of the 1960s? And is it true in a world overshadowed by global terrorism in the first decade of the third millennium?

A totally different but, perhaps, even more intriguing set of questions might be, would St Paul have been a fan of the Beatles? Would he have welcomed and applauded their popular song? Would he have felt that the four young lads from Liverpool had got close to the heart of the gospel, and confirmed the theme of his own great song of love contained in the first of his letters to the church at Corinth?

Whatever the answer to these questions might be, 'All you need is love' clearly touched a hidden chord in the hearts of ordinary people across the social spectrum, and rightly so, for love is of crucial importance in the growth to maturity and fulfilment of both individuals and communities. We cannot live without it. We cannot dispense with its services without diminishing ourselves and others. A community without love creates a vacuum that all too readily is filled with selfishness, contention and hatred.

We see national and international evidence of this on a daily basis, as images of racial, religious and sectarian violence flash across our television screens. We see it at the domestic level when families tear themselves apart through lack of love; and even the Church, whose members are commanded to love one another, frequently fails to live up to its own ideals, with appalling lapses of love as ecclesiastical dirty linen is washed in public. Individuals and groups, not content with disagreeing with one another, resort at best to point-scoring and at worst to character assassination.

Thankfully, this is not the whole story by any means. Love is stronger than hatred – and we also see evidence of this on a daily basis. For instance, areas of God's world that are scarred by violence often serve as a challenge to those whose selfless love and practical compassion takes them into the midst of the pain and conflict in order to help heal the wounds of hatred and build bridges of peace and reconciliation. And, despite the fact that it is not yet what God intends it to be, the same is true of the Church. Admittedly, it has been likened to a kindergarten where people are at their most childish, and to a hospital where people expose their wounds. But it is also a community into which God constantly pours his love in word, prayer and sacrament. It is a place where we learn to give ourselves in love to God and neighbour – a community of character. There is no greater influence within society than a community of people who are filled with the love of God and are giving practical expression to it. Such a community of love becomes the visible presence of the human Jesus, and a transforming influence in the world around.

It was the powerful and personified influence of that same love that changed Saul of Tarsus, as he was then known, from being a persecutor of the Church to being its greatest ambassador. It also provided the stimulus for his great song of love (1 Corinthians 13) that has challenged and inspired people across the ages. It was a love from which he couldn't escape, though he tried. It haunted him while he conspired to throw the followers of Jesus into prison. It convicted him as he willingly witnessed the stoning of Stephen, the first Christian martyr (Acts 7). Even as he struck fear into the heart of the infant Church, the transforming love of the crucified risen Jesus pierced his own heart in that amazing encounter on the Damascus road (Acts 9).

Small wonder, therefore, that love became a dominant theme of his life and work – a life and work of major significance in God's purposes for his Church and his world. Love was the fuel that fired his missionary endeavour. It was love that 'urged him on' (2 Corinthians 5.14), sometimes against impossible odds. And, far from taking it for granted, he never ceased to be amazed by God's love for him. You can almost hear the note of astonishment in his voice: 'the Son of God, who loved me and gave himself for me' (Galatians 2.20).

It is in the light of Paul's transforming experience of love, and by looking again at his superb song in 1 Corinthians 13 that I have felt constrained to write this little book. His memorable words and penetrating insights form what is, perhaps, the most popular and best known passage in the Bible. Its beauty is beyond question; its description of love is sublime. But I have found it to be a rather devastating document and am convinced that it should carry a health warning! For if we study it carefully and take it seriously, our life, and our relationship to other people, may never be quite the same again. Paul is shockingly blunt about those situations where love is missing (13.1–3). He is disturbingly precise and practical regarding the nature of love (13.4–7) and, in a unique way, he puts the whole of life in perspective as he reflects on the enduring quality of love (13.8–13).

I learned the words of the song by heart as a boy, and in a sense they have been part of my 'stock in trade' for over 50 years, but in recent days they have come to me with a freshness that is frightening and with a challenge that has rocked my status quo.

I hope, therefore, that the simple reflections which follow will convey that sense of freshness and challenge to my readers and enable them, with conviction and courage, to choose what Paul called 'the more excellent way' – the way of love. For love not only covers a multitude of sins; it also reflects the nature of God and brings us very close to his heart and mind.

1

Indispensable gift

Without love
I am a noisy gong or a clanging cymbal
...I am nothing...I gain nothing.

I had my first driving lesson when I was a young curate. At the end of it the instructor dropped me off at the churchyard with these words: 'Reverend sir, here endeth the first lesson. Learn quickly and learn well. You began at the churchyard; I don't want you to finish up there.' Ten weeks later he was in a state of extreme agitation, bordering on panic, as he pounded the pavement outside the driving test centre, believing that his worst fears had come to pass.

I had borrowed his car to take my test, which was scheduled to last 30 minutes, but 55 minutes after the examiner and I had set out there was still no sign of our return. Believe it or not, I had got lost while taking my driving test!

The examiner was new and unfamiliar with some of the local back streets. It resulted in what I can only describe as a 'Hampton Court maze' experience. After I had been driving for half an hour, I knew that something was wrong. I had been over the same route three times and still hadn't encountered any heavy traffic, while his instructions to me seemed increasingly hesitant and occasionally contradictory. Nevertheless, he kept his cool and remained courteous throughout, but when, an hour after we had started out, we arrived back at the test centre, I believe he was more relieved than I was. As I stopped the car and switched off the engine, he gave me an old-fashioned look and stared hard at my clerical collar. For one mad moment I thought he was going to make his confession. Instead, he smiled, signed the magic form and said, 'Congratulations, you've passed your driving test' – and gave me the certification to prove it! The little second-hand car that stood in my garage had been a gift, which I felt privileged to receive and proud to own. Now I could use it with authority and confidence, and to the delight of my young family.

It was an experience that readily came to mind as I began to take a fresh look at St Paul's song of love. It seems to me that this sublime passage of Scripture has many of the characteristics of a test certificate, adding authority to the use of spiritual gifts and helping to measure the quality and effectiveness of the life of the church in Corinth – or anywhere else for that matter.

Despite its problems, the local church in Corinth throbbed with life and vitality. It fulfilled Paul's vision of the Church as the body of Christ in which there are many members, each possessing a gift, or gifts, from God for use in building up the whole body towards maturity (1 Corinthians 12). In their enthusiasm to fulfil this idea, however, a spirit of rivalry developed among the members. Some became overzealous for the possession and practice of spectacular gifts. As a result, jealousy, arrogance and irritability came in and, it seems, love went out! So Paul had to remind them that, ultimately, the authenticity of their life in Christ would be measured not so much by the due exercise of gifts, but by the unmistakable evidence of love. He wanted the church, individually and corporately, to have the best that God could offer – to follow the more excellent way – so he challenged them, in strong and graphic terms, to take and pass the test of love. And the manner in which he challenged them was an example of the love which he declared to be indispensable.

An unflattering image

A good preacher always listens to his own sermons; after all, if he doesn't heed them, why should anyone else! So Paul, aware that he is about to say some very disagreeable things, does the humble and loving thing by speaking in hypothetical and personal terms. 'If I speak in the tongues of mortals and of angels, but do not have love, I am a noisy gong or a clanging cymbal.'

It is a fairly devastating self-assessment. The image of gong and cymbal conveys a shattering message to all who have ears to hear and the wisdom and courage to apply it to themselves. It comes as a shock to the system when those things in which we have taken great pride and invested so much significance are deemed to be worse than useless. It is disquieting when what was meant to be impressive and attractive instead becomes massively off-putting.

Paul's emphasis is clear. There is all the difference in the world between saying and doing. No matter how eloquent and impressive the tongues of mortals and angels may be, they are meaningless clamour, without love. Inspiring words are not enough; they are noise without heart. Among some members of that local church, the gift of 'tongues', namely, the ecstatic speech prompted by the Holy Spirit, was eagerly desired and highly rated. Indeed, Paul himself possessed the gift to a greater degree than most, so he certainly didn't despise speaking in tongues, but he kept it in perspective (1 Corinthians 14.18–19). If used in public worship when no interpreter was present, it revealed a lack of love towards strangers in the congregation. They would not understand it and would feel excluded by what was happening, hearing only noise but little meaning, sound but no sense.

But Paul's comments about the 'tongues of mortals and angels' are so general that it seems likely he was referring not only to ecstatic speech but also to ordinary speech. It too can be so devoid of love as to assault the ears but never reach the heart. Indeed, there are those whose eloquence can stir the emotions of others but do little more, because it lacks love. My homeland of Ulster, for instance, is not short of gifted orators, but throughout decades of sectarian troubles, some of the most stirring words have also been among the most strident and loveless. They too have resembled the noisy gong and the clanging cymbal.

However, before pointing the finger at others, perhaps, like Paul, we also might be prepared to put ourselves in the frame in this matter. It may be painful but necessary to reflect upon those occasions when we have impressed ourselves with our verbal dexterity and, at the same time, depressed others with our lack of love, thus doing more harm than good.

I cringe when I recall occasions, hopefully fewer than

4

I fear, when I have used people as 'pew fodder' over whom I have poured a torrent of words and ideas, boosting my own ego but doing little for their edification. No doubt there were times when I was guilty, metaphorically speaking, of 'banging the gong and clanging the cymbal' so loudly and insensitively that I succeeded only in making myself deaf to what others were trying to say to me.

Gongs and cymbals in the hands of a skilled percussionist, and as part of a large orchestra, can make a significant contribution to the majestic beauty of a musical presentation. On their own, however, they tend to produce sound without melody. The same is true of our speaking to others, whether in public or in private. It must pass the test of love, for without love, it is in danger of sounding hollow rather than harmonious.

All or nothing

The same test of love needed to be applied to four other aspects of the life of Christians in Corinth for, as Paul reminds himself and them: 'And if I have prophetic powers, and understand all mysteries and all knowledge, and if I have all faith, so as to remove mountains, but do not have love, I am nothing' (13.2). That is a fairly extraordinary and potentially rather disturbing statement. To possess just one of the four gifts mentioned here would qualify most people for a valued place in the life of any local church, but to possess all four and still miss out seems an awful waste of talent.

Though each may have a particular nuance of meaning, there is coordination among the first three of this important quartet of gifts; they all depend on the revelation of God. Through the proper exercise of these gifts, God makes known to us those things we could never find out for ourselves. The person who is gifted by God with prophetic powers, or knowledge, or the understanding of mysteries, is able, as it were, to draw back the curtain, allowing us a glimpse into the mind and purposes of God. In this connection, Paul gives a special place to prophecy and considers it vital in building up the church (1 Corinthians 14.4).

So often it is the wise and faithful exercise of these gifts that moves the Church forward and enables it to grow towards maturity in Christ. It is an endowment not restricted to church leaders. I have seen evidence of it in the life of a godly widow who, with humility, brought words from God into the barrenness of a local church situation. Internal strife had hardened its spiritual arteries and stunted its growth. Through her, the revealed word of God broke the deadlock, prompted repentance and released a flow of love into the surrounding community.

In the light of such things, the implication of Paul's words seems all the more startling. He is saying, 'Though I may speak words God has given me to say, and I know everything there is to know about his secret truths and hidden purposes, if I do not have love, I am nothing.' And the same point is hammered home in the final element of the quartet: 'If I have all faith, so as to remove mountains, but do not have love, I am nothing.' He is not referring to that faith which is the very basis of our life in Christ, but to the special gift of faith which is given to some, but not to all (1 Corinthians 12.9). He has in mind the kind of person who has such confidence in the power of God that they are not put off by being told that something cannot be done. On the contrary, such negative sentiments simply act as an incentive for them to attempt and achieve the impossible. The Church would be the poorer without the persistent vision and the unshakeable commitment of those with the gift of 'miracle-working' faith. Yet, even here, Paul insists, 'If I have all faith, so as to remove mountains, but do not have love, I am nothing.'

Paul's perception is devastating. And though once more he speaks in personal terms, thus allowing his own life and ministry to be subjected to the test of love, the implication for others is clear. Those in the church who see themselves as important because they possess the highest gifts in the fullest measure, yet lack love, are not important at all. They are nothing.

A poor bargain

Paul has not yet completed the opening challenge of his song of love. There is an even more incisive and astonishing comment to come, one which he applies to the very highest qualities of human life, namely charity towards others and the sacrifice of oneself. Most of us would assume that acts of mercy and the acceptance of martyrdom could only be motivated by love, but Paul asks us to think again. 'If I give away all my possessions, and if I hand over my body so that I may boast, but do not have love, I gain nothing.' I strike a poor bargain.

Paul knew that generosity and self-sacrifice are at the heart of the gospel he lived and preached. He knew also that open-handed, self-giving devotion on our part, if it is a reflection of God's undeserved generosity in Christ, contains the very essence of love. Nevertheless, he was aware that grand dramatic gestures, without love, are also possible. And, if we are honest with ourselves, we know he was right. Self-love can be very deceitful, especially in this matter of giving our possessions. It can convince us, for instance, that our motives are pure, even when a spirit of ostentation or a desire for self-justification is really calling the tune. Paul insists, therefore, on applying the test of love to actions that some would consider to be beyond question. He was wise to do so.

I vividly recall the mayor of a major city asking me for support when summoned to meet a so-called prominent philanthropist, who was offering financial help following a local tragedy. The mayor was intimidated by the man's powerful and insistent demand that he be allowed to solve the problem, and believed it to be a desire for personal publicity. Later events proved that the mayor's instincts were correct. A longing for publicity rather than a love for people was at the heart of his selfish ambition. Public generosity was being practised for self-aggrandizement and private gain.

It was a recollection of this incident that enabled me to appreciate the New Revised Standard Version of Paul's words: 'And if I hand over my body so that I may boast, but do not have love, I gain nothing.' The words 'so that I may boast' replace the traditional phrase 'to be burned'. I was brought up on the traditional version and it is certainly the more dramatic, though some biblical scholars suggest that the phrase, 'that I may boast', more accurately reflects the situation pertaining at the time Paul wrote.

But, whatever translation we prefer, it will strike a contemporary note for us today. We live in days when a terrorist, responsible for the untimely death of many others, who gives his own body up to death, through hunger strike or suicide bomb, is proclaimed to be a martyr, idolized by thousands. This frightening development within today's world was underlined by a television interview I watched recently. Visiting a Palestinian refugee camp, the TV reporter asked a group of beautiful, intelligent and bright-eyed school children the age-old question, 'What do you want to be when you grow up?' They replied with one voice, 'Martyrs!'

Such things give an unexpected relevance to Paul's words, the implication of which remain unchanged and unequivocal. The giving of my possessions to others, and my body for a cause, may be motivated by many factors, but if love is absent I gain nothing.

The vital ingredient

Paul's words, 'I am nothing', and 'I gain nothing', may at first sound a little strange. If my motives are pure, then my giving to others, whether in terms of using my spiritual gifts or sharing my material possessions, should be for their benefit rather than mine. Surely, the fact that 'I gain nothing' should not surprise me. Ought I to be looking for personal reward? Would this not put me in the same category as the flamboyant philanthropist mentioned above?

To think in this way, however, is to misunderstand the import of Paul's words. They are concerned not with absence of reward, but with poverty of character. In his superb song, he sees love as distinct from all the other gifts he has listed, because it has to do with the individual's character. Love is the power that transforms our character. What concerned Paul, therefore, was that though he might be immensely endowed with spiritual gifts that impressed others, it did him no good if, through lack of love, he failed to reveal the likeness of Christ and the character of God.

He has indicated (13.1–3) that it is only too possible to experience and express spiritual gifts without love. By the same token (13.4–7), he implies that it is impossible to experience the love, which reflects the character of God without expressing that same love through our own character, in words and actions. To lack love not only reveals the poverty-stricken nature of our own Christian character, it is also a sad distortion of the grace of God, whose character of love we are called to reflect. Such lack of love does us no good, nor does it glorify God, for love has its source in God.

This is the reason why the word love was given such prominence in Paul's vocabulary. Of the 116 times the word appears in the New Testament, nearly two-thirds of them occur in his writings. It carried such importance for him because it opened the heart of the gospel he preached and the heart of the God he worshipped and served – and it was no ordinary word!

There was a variety of words for love available to New Testament writers. Nevertheless, they seemed reluctant to use most of them, and for good reason. The highest concept of love those words conveyed tended to be selective, emotional and dependent on the lovable qualities it saw in the object of the person concerned. Instead they opted for the virtually unknown word, *agape*, to which they attached rich significance.

Far from being selective, it was universal. It described a love that operates when it is neither attracted nor reciprocated. It doesn't depend on a worthy object;

indeed, it is a love for the utterly unworthy, because it arises from the character of the lover. It is the love that proceeds from God, whose very essence is love; a love that, according to Paul, is part of the transforming experience of every Christian disciple, for 'God proves his love for us in that while we still were sinners Christ died for us' (Romans 5.8). It is the selfless, self-giving, sacrificial love, seen to perfection in the life and work of Christ, and which Christians are called to share, however imperfectly, with others.

For this privileged yet demanding task we are not left to our own devices. We have an infinite resource available, because 'God's love has been poured into our hearts through the Holy Spirit who has been given to us' (Romans 5.5). If in any of our work for God, love is missing, we are clearly not in step with his Spirit, for, as someone has said, 'Love is the inner compulsion of God's Spirit coming to concrete expression in loving word and act.'

Some aspects of that practical expression of love will form the basis of the chapters that follow. And as we read them we may discover that we are not only studying the words of Paul, but following in the footsteps of Jesus along the path of love.

2

Strength held in restraint

Love is patient; love is kind.

James and John had a short fuse. Jesus, fortunately, had not. On the occasion when the brothers had lived up to their name as 'sons of thunder', he placed a restraining hand upon them and saved them from folly.

The occasion was a proposed visit by Jesus to a Samaritan village (Luke 9.51–56). He had sent some disciples ahead to make the necessary arrangements for his coming, but they met with a frosty response. The inhabitants of the village had no intention of welcoming what they perceived as a group of Jewish pilgrims on their way to Jerusalem, even if Jesus was among them. They refused him hospitality.

To say that James and John were 'miffed' would be a massive understatement. They were furious and their reaction was petulant and cruel. In modern jargon, they wanted to 'zap' the village, saying to Jesus, 'Lord, do you want us to command fire to come down from heaven and consume them?'

Whatever their motivation for such drastic action, they were out of order and Jesus told them so. To invoke the power of God in order to crush people who have upset us was totally foreign to the character of Jesus. A similar admonition was given to those disciples who tried to defend him with the sword at the time of his arrest in the Garden of Gethsemane. 'No more of this!', he told them, rebuking their aggression and healing the physical injury they had caused. That was not the way he had chosen to do the work of God.

It wasn't that he lacked strength; on the contrary, as he reminded them, 'Do you think that I cannot appeal to my Father, and he will at once send me more than twelve legions of angels?' (Matthew 26.53). No. He had deliberately set aside the unprincipled use of power. His strength was held in restraint because that was the way he had chosen, a way that reflected the character of God.

Paul had a similar conviction. So when, in his song of love, he describes how love acts in everyday life, he begins by speaking of patience and kindness. 'Love is patient'. Love is strength held in restraint.

Victory over just resentment

For nearly five years I was privileged, and humbled, to observe love's self-restraint in the life and work of Michael, a relatively young and extremely talented priest. He was surprised, and many of his peers were annoyed, when he was asked to accept a senior leadership task within the church. Some felt he was too young for the job, others claimed he had 'jumped the queue', and a few were bitter that he had been chosen in preference to them. Michael, despite his natural reticence at being thrust into a leadership role, believed it to be a call from God, and in obedience to him and the desire of the church, said 'yes'.

It wasn't an easy decision and initially it didn't have a comfortable outcome. A few people, who should have known better, nursed a strong resentment against him. Their feelings were largely hidden but behind the scenes they pursued a policy, currently common in politics, of 'briefing' against him. They sowed seeds of doubt about his competence and attributed false statements to him. Most people were angry at such unfair and at times unscrupulous behaviour but Michael, aware of what was going on, remained passive and peaceful about it. He had the wisdom to know that to respond in kind, by fighting fire with fire, would only produce greater conflagration, and bring harm to church and gospel. He followed the pathway of patience.

There were times, however, when that patience was sorely tried – public occasions when his detractors, in their desire to embarrass and entrap him, descended almost to the level of the gutter, much to the distress and resentment of others, but not Michael. He had just cause to feel resentful. The persistent and insidious criticism of the few must have been a burden to him, and could have been a constant hindrance to his work for God. He was a person of considerable intelligence and eloquence. He had the mental and verbal ability to crush his opponents by showing them up in public and destroying their credibility. Instead, he treated them with courtesy and calmness. He met their ill-disguised resentment with loving self-restraint which, over the months, created a situation where enemies learned to respect him and friends were humbled by his unshakeable patience.

In the New Testament, the word for patience is always used with reference to people rather than circumstances. It is used to describe those who, despite having been provoked and wronged, refuse to repay evil with evil, but instead repay evil with good.

Michael was a classic, high-profile example of patience, but he didn't have a monopoly on it. Thankfully, patience, which Paul refers to as a 'fruit of the Spirit' (Galatians 5.22), is a reality that is present in the lives of many ordinary people. If it were not so, life would be more fraught and less interesting. I thank God every day for the patience others have shown me over the years. As I was the youngest of 14 children, my mother's patience should have been exhausted by the time I arrived. But it wasn't, far from it. She lived until she was 90 and nothing fazed her. Her patience was immeasurable and invariably cheerful. Sadly, not all of it rubbed off on me, but I learned enough to know that much more is achieved by patience than by power. Alongside our retrospective appreciation of others, we might like to add a touch of current realism about ourselves. We can be so busy complaining about those who try our patience, and whom we consider to be a blessed nuisance, that we can easily forget that there are others who consider us in a similar light!

Patience has been called 'the queen of virtues'. Be that as it may; wherever, in the face of provocation, patience is expressed, the negative attitudes of others are negated. Wherever true, self-restraining patience is found, there is the reality of love.

A *divine reality*

It is a reality that finds its source in God. The attitude of God and of Christ towards people is the model upon which the patience of love is founded. The whole history of God's dealings with his people is dominated by his generous and gracious treatment of them, despite their rebellion and stubbornness. He didn't turn a blind eye to their idolatry and sin, frequently warning them about the self-inflicted consequences of their actions, but neither did he lash out at the sins of his people. He exercised restraint. He was 'slow to anger' and, even when discipline was administered, it was always for their ultimate good. He refused to cast them off or let them go. His patience was enduring: 'The Lord is not slow about his promise, as some think of slowness, but is patient with you, not wanting any to perish, but all to come to repentance' (2 Peter 3.9).

This enduring patience of God was seen to perfection in the life and work of Jesus. In his beautiful story of the prodigal son, for instance, he reveals, through the character of the waiting father, the incredible generosity of a God who never ceases to love, forgive and restore those whose foolishness has got them into trouble (Luke 15.11–32). Even in the shadow of the cross, when the powers of evil were threatening to overwhelm him, there was an astonishing response of selfless restraint. There was o vengeful, violent outburst against evil. He exposed evil not by denouncing it, but by allowing it to do its worst and, through his suffering, sacrificial love, negating its power.

If we had been writing the script for the story of the cross and resurrection, the 'good guy' would have emerged from the tomb on the third day to give the 'bad guys' their come-uppance with a powerful display of revenge. Thank God, he wrote the script and not us, for his thoughts are not our thoughts; nor are his ways our ways (see Isaiah 55.8). Renewal rather than revenge was the keynote of God's script: 'The God of our ancestors raised up Jesus, whom you had killed by hanging him on a tree. God exalted him at his right hand as Leader and Saviour, so that he might give repentance to Israel and forgiveness of sins' (Acts 5.30–31).

This gracious and patient attitude of God is most beautifully expressed in the words of F. W. Faber's memorable hymn:

> For the love of God is broader
> Than the measure of man's mind;
> And the heart of the Eternal
> Is most wonderfully kind.

A positive partner

Patience and kindness go hand in hand. Time and again in the Scriptures, they are linked together. They stand side by side among 'the fruit of the Spirit' (Galatians 5.22), and are partners in giving practical expression to the love that Paul exalts in his song and commends to the church. The active kindness of love is an ideal companion to the more passive patience of love. If the patience of love describes the self-restraint of long-suffering, the kindness of love describes the 'doing good' to those who do us wrong. It speaks of putting ourselves at the service of others – even of those who set out to make life difficult for us.

It is easier said than done, of course. If people are giving us a tough time, unfairly, the natural reaction of many if not most of us is not to take it lying down but to hit back hard. In this respect I recall, with both humour and horror, having to act as referee and reconciler one Sunday evening. A black congregation used a local community centre for their worship services. Enthusiasm was a keynote of their gatherings, and late on Sunday evenings, the sound of music and singing set the feet tapping or the nerve-ends screaming, depending where you lived.

Sandra lived next door. Indeed, her house shared a wall with the community centre – oh dear! Though she was a devout Christian, she reached the stage where patience was exhausted and kindness was the last thing she had in mind. Acting on behalf of other disgruntled neighbours, she hired some extremely powerful hi-fi equipment. Placing the massive loudspeakers against the 'shared' wall, she 'hit back' by blasting the worshippers next door with a selection of music guaranteed to have the maximum effect. She did, at least, keep the music vaguely religious, by including Tom Jones' rendition of 'Delilah' and a thunderous version of the Battle Hymn of the Republic!

Unfortunately, Sandra's efforts were interpreted as one church persecuting another, and for a while the peace of the neighbourhood and the unity of the Christian community was threatened. At the end of the day, disaster was averted by an act of loving kindness – and common sense. The local Anglican church building was offered to the black congregation for their worship services, which were rescheduled for Sunday afternoon. Peace reigned and the kindness of love triumphed. But it was a close thing.

Absolutely right and utterly wrong

Sandra was absolutely right to respond to the insensitive intrusion into her private space, but she was totally wrong in the manner of that response. Good-quality earplugs might have been a less contentious option, but it wouldn't have produced the same result as the act of hospitality on the part of the local church.

Therein lies the true significance of what Paul meant by kindness. We are to serve others, including those we consider objectionable, not in order to build up a glowing reputation for ourselves, but in order that what we do might ultimately lead to them being blessed.

That was certainly the attitude of Jesus. He wanted us to respond positively to those who would do us harm. We are not required to sit still and do nothing in the face of insult and wrong. He urged us to repay them – with practical works of kindness and love; in other words, to surprise them with grace, to repay evil with good. He put the point graphically in the Sermon on the Mount: 'You have heard that it was said, "You shall love your neighbour and hate your enemy." But I say to you, love your enemies and pray for those who persecute you' (Matthew 5.43–44). In following this way of kindness, or surprising grace, that we reveal that we are children of God, 'for he is kind to the ungrateful and the wicked' (Luke 6.35).

To be god-like in our attitude towards others is the challenge Paul places before us, just as he placed it before the Christians in Corinth. Patience and kindness, as expressions of the love of God, are as urgently needed today as they ever were. There will be those, of course, who will see such things as weak and ineffective in witnessing to a modern and rather aggressive society. In such an environment, some might say that to hold strength in restraint is a waste of energy. Paul, from his own experience, would disagree. He learned the hard way that 'power is made perfect in weakness' (2 Corinthians 12.9).

Patience and kindness, far from being a waste of energy, provide a release of productive energy that not only has its source in God, but also reflects his love.

3

A healthy attitude

Love is not envious or boastful
or arrogant or rude.

The dietician stood, ominously, at the foot of my hospital bed. A sylphlike figure, she looked the picture of health and personified the message she was about to deliver. A few hours earlier, my cardiologist had been blunt and uncompromising: 'Get your weight down and your walking up to five miles a day.' My dietician was equally forthright, but prefaced her words with a shy smile: 'Reverend, there are certain things you must avoid if you are to prevent further heart disease and a serious curtailment of your life and work.'

Her message was clear and concise. It went something like this: 'chocolate – bad, fruit – good; fish and chips – dreadful, salads – wonderful; sherry trifle – risky, plain yoghurt – safe!' It disapproved of virtually everything I liked to eat and gave star rating to some things I loathed. But I knew it made sense. I also knew that my taste buds would need some convincing. Nevertheless, I accepted the force of her contention that, for the sake of my health, certain culinary delights must be avoided.

Paul's contention regarding love had similar force. He was concerned about the spiritual health of the congregation in Corinth, and wanted them to measure it in the same way as he assessed the value of his own ministry, by the presence and reality of love. So, having told them how love acts – 'Love is patient; love is kind' – he spells out what love must avoid: 'Love is not envious or boastful or arrogant or rude.' He doesn't produce this list of negatives at random, off the top of his head, as it were. It reflected the state of affairs among some in the congregation at Corinth, whose attitude towards themselves and others was not always symptomatic of spiritual health and vigour. It was indicative of some 'dis-ease' at the heart of that Christian community (2 Corinthians 12.20).

Distorted desire

The challenge of each of the words on the list, and the attitudes they represent, are not restricted to their immediate context. They have a contemporary ring about them. If we are honest, most of us will have recognized their appearance, from time to time, within our local church and, sadly, within our own lives.

This is certainly true of envy, though we need to be careful of the meaning we attach to the word. As he prepared to launch into his song of love, Paul used the Greek verb 'to envy' in a good sense, to encourage the Christians in Corinthian to aim high: 'Eagerly desire the greater gifts' (1 Corinthians 12.31, NIV). Clearly there is nothing wrong with striving to be the best for God; after all, that is the theme of his song, to follow the more excellent way of love. And there are times when we all use the word envy in an innocent, even commendable, manner. When, for instance, we say to a friend who is bravely enduring severe illness, 'I envy you your courage,' it is not usually an indication of bitter jealousy but rather of admiration and love.

However, that is not the most common meaning of the word 'envy' in the writings of Paul, and when he says, 'Love is not envious', there is certainly nothing to admire in the attitude the word conveys. It carries the meaning of a strong, passionate and consuming jealousy. Indeed, it suggests a grudging attitude towards the possessions that others have, allied to a strong and selfish desire that we had them instead! Such envy contains a pernicious element of meanness. It speaks of a distorted desire that is incompatible with love, for love takes pleasure in the success of others.

It is this ability to be pleased when others are successful that provides another yardstick of the reality of love in our lives. Are we delighted at the prosperity and good fortune of other people, including our friends? When we hear people singing the praises of a colleague or friend, of whom we may be secretly jealous, do we pull a face or ostentatiously place a hand over our mouth? Such silent actions speak volumes about us, as well as suggesting to others that they don't know what we know about the person concerned and, perhaps, their praises are misdirected. Envy takes many forms, but I believe this to be one of the most subtle and pernicious.

But envy, in any shape or form, is a complete waste of energy. Monica Furlong, the feminist writer, said, 'If envy was not such a tearing thing to feel, it would be the most comic of sins. It is usually, if not always, based on a complete misunderstanding of another person's situation.' Those are perceptive words, the truth of which is reflected in the experience of most of us. Have there not been times when, viewed from a distance, the situation of another person has seemed so impressive and attractive that we have found ourselves longing to be like them and, perhaps, resentful that we weren't? Yet, the closer we have got to them, the more we have discovered that things were not as they appeared. Smiling faces were hiding broken hearts. The affluence of success was disguising an impoverished spirit, and a ready repartee was concealing deep despair. Perhaps, in the light of these things, our uninformed envy was replaced by compassionate understanding, if not pity.

The truth is that envy, if not overruled by love, can result in a distorted desire that destroys relationships and creates havoc within communities. We need, therefore, constantly to remind ourselves of Paul's words to the Christians in Philippi: 'Do nothing from selfish ambition or conceit, but in humility regard others as better than yourselves' (Philippians 2.3).

Self-advertisement

The opposite of the self-effacement Paul commends is self-advertisement, which he claims is irreconcilable with love. 'Love is not boastful'. It doesn't brag. It doesn't make a name for itself at the expense of others. Once again, it is interesting how, in the mind of Paul, love is personified. He speaks of it in terms of reality – not dormant or passive, but alive and active – the reality of God's gracious activity on our behalf. This is seen, for instance, in the life and work of the crucified Christ, who didn't put his own interests first but gave himself for others. 'For you know the generous act of our Lord Jesus Christ, that though he was rich, yet for your sakes he became poor, so that by his poverty you might become rich' (2 Corinthians 8.9). Boasting is inconsistent with that kind of love, as Paul reminded some Christians in Corinth, who were claiming personal merit for gifts given them by the grace of God. 'What do you have that you did not receive? And if you received it, why do you boast as though it were not a gift?' (1 Corinthians 4.7).

We need to be very careful in this matter of boasting for, as we know, pride often comes before a fall, as Peter painfully discovered. When Jesus had warned his followers that all would desert him in his hour of need, Peter boasted, 'Even though all become deserters, I will not' (Mark 14.29). In other words, you can depend on me. I'm no coward. I can cope with pressure. We know the sad outcome of such a sincere, if opinionated, claim. Peter not only deserted Jesus; he denied him three times (Mark 14.66–72).

An unhappy and unedifying aspect of Peter's boasting was the manner in which, perhaps unconsciously, he diminished his fellow disciples by comparing them unfavourably with himself – putting them in a different category. 'Even though all become deserters, I will not.' They might be a bit 'wobbly', but I won't. I'm different. This is one of the unfortunate spin-offs from careless boasting. The more we boastfully place ourselves in the spotlight, the more we run the risk of casting others into the shadows.

It was being on the reverse side of that particular dichotomy, if I may speak with tongue in cheek, that led to my long-standing aversion to clergy conferences. I almost always came away from such gatherings feeling depressed. No doubt the fault lay in my self-pity or warped perception, but, as I listened to some of my colleagues tell their stories, everyone else seemed to be doing better than I. Their parishes were more successful, their preaching was more effective, their impact on the community was more powerful, or at least that was the impression being given. Sinner that I am, I took comfort in the thought that, perhaps, their imagination was also more fertile than mine!

Seriously, though, we need to be careful lest, in building up our own reputation, we are guilty of undervaluing the reputation of others. Love puts the interests of others before its own (Philippians 2.4). Boasting about ourselves and our achievements is inappropriate, for we have nothing that we have not received. However, there is every reason to boast of the one by whose grace we have received so much. With this in mind, Paul encourages us to boast in Christ. 'Let the one who boasts, boast in the Lord' (1 Corinthians 1.31). Isaac Watts had the same idea when he wrote:

> When I survey the wondrous Cross
>   On which the Prince of Glory died,
> My richest gain I count but loss,
>   And pour contempt on all my pride.
>
> Forbid it, Lord, that I should boast
>   Save in the Cross of Christ my God;
> All the vain things that charm me most,
>   I sacrifice them to his Blood.

Self-convincing

If self-centred boasting is inappropriate, so also is arrogance. 'Love is not arrogant'. There may not be a vast difference in meaning between them but, in my mind, arrogance is the least acceptable face of boastfulness. It refers to someone who is 'puffed up' with an exaggerated sense of their own importance. 'Big-headed' is the colloquial way of saying that such a person is conceited but, however we may describe them, they believe themselves to be a cut above the rest.

For my part, as an amateur student of human nature, I have come to the conclusion that arrogant people are those who are convinced by the content of their own boasting. It seems to be a quirk of human nature that the more we hear ourselves saying something, the more likely we are to believe it, whether it is true or not. This is particularly the case if people massage our ego by responding to our boasting with admiration and envy. If we have convinced ourselves that in comparison with others we are special, if not unique, then an attitude of arrogance is not far away – though love may be.

Such a view is not mere theory. It is based on experience. Marcus was an active and gifted lay person within his local church. Contemporary spirituality was his great theme, and he developed a reputation as a local guru on the subject. Humility, however, was not one of his many gifts. Perceived as the expert on spirituality, he began to proclaim himself as such, and rather ostentatiously offered his expertise far and wide.

His clientele grew. But so also did his ego and, sadly, his arrogance. He began to believe his own spin, that his was the authoritative voice of spirituality within the region. He started to make claims that were unbiblical and unsustainable; indeed, he decided to write his own rules. Sadly, to use modern terminology, he lost the plot, but not his arrogance. He ran off with another man's wife, and when confronted with the sinfulness of his actions he showed no remorse, claiming instead that 'they were on a spiritual journey'. The more he repeated it, the more he believed it, even though he left a trail of havoc and hurt in his wake.

Arrogance is not only incompatible with love; it can also drastically distort our view of ourselves and our Lord. It did so in the case of Marcus, and was an issue that threatened the life of the congregation in Corinth. Cliques had developed in the church, each attaching itself to a favourite teacher and declaring, 'I belong to Paul', or 'I belong to Apollos', or 'I belong to Cephas', or 'I belong to Christ'. They were causing serious division in the church because they were arrogantly allying themselves to a leader of their own choice and, or so it seemed, giving him hero status. They even turned Christ into a party figure. Paul would have none of it and, with devastating logic and a series of pointed questions, he put them in their proper place and restored Christ to his (1 Corinthians 1.10–17).

His words are a salutary warning to those who, even today, divide and disfigure the Church with party strife. Arrogance can destroy unity, cause us to get ourselves and Christ out of focus, and hinder the mission of God. Love is the antidote in such circumstances, for 'love is not arrogant'.

Behaving properly

Finally, in this quartet of things that love avoids, we are reminded that 'love is not rude'. Older translations expressed it more quaintly: 'Charity doth not behave itself unseemly', that is, love does not behave improperly. Since love has its source in God, it needs to behave in a way that reflects God's character. Any lack of graciousness in our attitude to others, therefore, may reflect not only an absence of love but also an unfaithfulness to God.

Within Paul's immediate context, of course, some of the hairstyles of both men and women were, according to current cultural convention, considered unseemly and the cause of offence. Among more serious matters, however, was the presence of gluttony and drunkenness at the Eucharist and signs of immorality within the membership. In connection with these issues, I can imagine there were some red faces in the assembly when Paul's letter was first read.

Again, however, it would be a mistake to limit the application of Paul's words to the immediate circumstances in Corinth. The phrase 'is not rude' has a wide range of meaning and can be applied with equal force today because, in essence, it requires us not to treat people improperly or unfairly. In all our relationships, whether in business or in pleasure, in the church or in the home, in public or in private, we must not deal with people in the wrong way.

Most of us will recognize unseemly behaviour when it reveals itself in immoral, dishonest, dishonourable or indecent conduct, and readily acknowledge that it is wrong. At the same time we might be blind to, or ignore, behaviour that is unfair and improper. The cruel jibe, for instance, that publicly humiliates another person. The serious yet untrue accusation, made when the accused is not present, that results in character assassination. The unfriendly look, or turn of the head, that unmistakably says, 'You are not welcome among us.' Love does not behave in this way.

Jack was known as a 'character'. He had a reputation for speaking his mind and not suffering fools gladly. Blunt and bellicose described him perfectly. He gloried in his reputation and worked hard to maintain it. Those who were able gave him no quarter and returned his belligerence with interest. Others had the capacity to laugh at him and say, 'I see you've got out of the wrong side of the bed again, Jack.' A few, more gentle, souls, however, suffered his blunt and sometimes barbed comments in silence, and went back to the loneliness of their home mentally and emotionally bruised and hurting. Jack undoubtedly *was* a character, but the question that needs to be asked in such a situation is, Does love behave in this way? Does such behaviour reflect the graciousness of God?

'Love is not envious or boastful or arrogant or rude.' Love invites and enables us to avoid these things in order to promote a healthy attitude towards ourselves and others, through which we reflect the graciousness of God.

4

Generous contentment

Love does not insist on its own way;
it is not irritable or resentful.

Geordies are top of the happiness league. That was the conclusion reached by a recent national survey. However seriously or light-heartedly we were meant to take the results, the north-east of England was declared to be the place where most happiness is found. An expert, when asked to comment, was very diplomatic, saying that he was sure the north-east didn't have a monopoly on happiness. He was also firm in the conviction that material possessions didn't produce lasting happiness – winning the Lottery often produced more problems than it solved – but that other things, like good friends, were a major factor. In his opinion, the essence of happiness is 'long-term contentment'. In other words, though external circumstances may play a part, the secret of lasting happiness seems to lie within ourselves and our own inner resources.

Paul expressed a similar view in his personal testimony to the Christians at Philippi: 'I have learned to be content with whatever I have' (Philippians 4.11). Cynics might reply, 'You must be joking. Given the changing circumstances of life, no one can be universally content.' But that is exactly what Paul claims. He says, 'In any and all circumstances I have learned the secret of being well-fed and of going hungry, of having plenty and of being in need. I can do all things through him who strengthens me' (Philippians 4.12–13). He had gained confidence through experience. He had been an unhappy, discontented person until faith in Christ became part of his inner resources. Then he seemed able to cope with whatever life threw at him. His independence in the face of life's circumstances arose from his dependence on Christ.

It was his experience of Christ-centred inner resources, which included the love of God poured into our hearts by the Holy Spirit (Romans 5.5), that enabled him to encourage the Christians in Corinth to reveal not simply stoical endurance, but generous contentment, in the face of various trials. He gives three examples of how love reacts in such circumstances: 'Love does not insist on its own way; it is not irritable or resentful'.

Me first

'Love does not insist on its own way' is a memorable principle, encapsulating the unselfish attitude required of those who follow Christ. It was the principle which shaped his life and work. 'I have come down from heaven,' he said, 'not to do my own will, but the will of him who sent me' (John 6.38). To live our lives without always seeking our own advantage is a challenging and acceptable aspect of belonging to Christ.

But, in a society where the rights of individuals and groups are trumpeted, and increasingly considered sacrosanct, the principle is not just memorable; it is positively subversive. It overturns and undermines the conventional wisdom that in a competitive world we should promote our own interest at the expense of others. If the principle 'love does not insist on its own way' was universally applied by Christians, it would revolutionize the life of many churches. Even church committees might seem like a foretaste of heaven if demanding and insistent self-interest gave way to a genuine and corporate search for the mind of Christ.

All too often, however, even in Christian circles, there is a dogmatism that insists that our way is best and consequently all other ways are suspect. And it isn't always deep theological issues that cause disharmony. I have known church committees bitterly divided over the choice of hymn tunes and, in one classic case, over whether or not the Harvest Supper would be vegetarian!

Strangely enough, it was the question of non-vegetarian food that threatened the unity and effectiveness of the church in Corinth, and almost certainly caused Paul to include this great principle in his song of love. Meat offered to idols was at the heart of the conflict (1 Corinthians 10.23—11.1). Some Christians had no compunction about going to the local market and buying meat that may have been offered to idols. They had no scruples about it because they considered idols as nothing. Other Christians, however, if they knew the meat had been offered to idols, refused to eat it and were offended by those who did. The trouble was that each group became so focused on its own need that it couldn't see the other's point of view, and resorted to throwing insults at its opponents. Paul, who had no scruples about eating such meat, does not act to his own advantage, but sees the way forward in terms of love, which puts the interest of others before his own: 'I try to please everyone in everything I do, not seeking my own advantage, but that of many' (1 Corinthians 10.33).

Though idol meat was a serious issue in the early days of the Church, to modern minds it must seem bizarre – just how some rules and regulations of today's church must appear to outsiders. Nevertheless, it touches on a current issue, regarding rights and responsibilities, that presses heavily upon both church and society. I am not talking about basic human rights, like dignity, respect, justice, and the provision of housing, food, water and health care, which Christians must be in the forefront of seeking for all those in need, especially in the developing countries. What I have in mind is the incessant and vociferous demand in society for 'my rights' over against those of other people, coupled with an almost total silence regarding 'my responsibilities' towards other people. The culture of complaint that pervades much of modern society may spring largely from the current imbalance between rights and responsibilities, which lays greater emphasis on individualism than it does on community.

Love subverts this prevailing climate. It is neither self-seeking nor self-important. It doesn't seek its own ends nor demand its own rights, but is concerned about the rights of others. Indeed, a careful study of that controversy about meat offered to idols reveals that the love of which Paul speaks is prepared to give up, for the sake of others, the very thing to which it is entitled. It was this kind of love and mindset that was demonstrated so astonishingly by Jesus, and described and commended by Paul:

> Let the same mind be in you that was in Christ Jesus,
> who, though he was in the form of God,
> > did not regard equality with God
> > as something to be exploited,
> but emptied himself,
> > taking the form of a slave,
> > being born in human likeness.
> And being found in human form,
> > he humbled himself
> > and became obedient to the point of
> > > death –
> > even death on a cross.
>
> > > > > > > (Philippians 2.5–8)

That kind of love puts rights and responsibilities in perspective.

Under control

That kind of love also keeps in perspective those who, for whatever reason, have a tendency to drive us up the walls with exasperation. 'Love is not irritable'.

In an attempt to clarify the meaning of the word 'irritable', within its context, some have used a different word or phrase, for example, 'Love never flies into a temper' (Barclay), 'is not easily angered' (NIV), 'is not touchy' (Phillips). In the end they amount to the same thing. When faced with provocation or exasperation, love does not lose control of itself or react in a way that makes the situation worse. It doesn't 'fly off the handle' with words and actions that it later regrets. It deals graciously with the cause of the irritation and smooths the pathway for continuing constructive relationships.

I believe that this is close to what Paul had in mind when he says 'Love is not irritable', but I also believe that it is not as easy as it sounds – I speak with a self-conscious awareness of my Irish temperament! But I also speak as a Christian, who is prepared to admit that there are times when unfailing serenity in the face of persistent irritation, though by no means impossible, is not always easy.

To some extent, it may depend upon our personality type. Some are unflappable in the face of extreme provocation. Others become touchy over the least irritation. Most of us are somewhere in between, and all of us will recognize that there are situations when it would be wrong not to be angry. When, for instance, we are faced with the injustice that blatantly denies human rights and condemns people to distress and poverty, it is entirely proper that we should be angry on their behalf. But we serve them best if our anger is kept under control and its energy channelled into positive action for their deliverance.

Nevertheless, the import of the principle remains, and cannot be ignored: 'Love is not irritable'. In rising to its challenge, however, we must be careful lest, in claiming more for the principle than it claims for itself, we end up totally discouraged. It is a fact of life that people and things get on our nerves. In my pastoral ministry, I came to the conclusion that I must never ask the question 'How are you?' unless I was prepared to listen to the answer. My sensitivity arose, not from any innate

38

goodness, but from painful past encounters with those who had answered the question at great length and in massive detail – leaving my nerves in shreds. Those who insist on telling me how gifted they are and how wonderfully God is using them have a similar effect upon me. What they say may be gloriously true but, sinner that I am, the manner in which they tell the story threatens to bring out the worst in me.

These are two examples of the kind of thing that can produce irritation in everyday life. There are more serious challenges to our serenity of spirit than these, of course, and all of us will have our own horror stories to tell. I was interested, therefore, to discover how Paul coped when things or people threatened to get on his nerves. Take, for instance, the disappointment he must have felt at the development of party spirit within the church (1 Corinthians 1.10–17). Then there was the constant questioning of his authority and integrity, shown in their criticism of his failure to visit them (2 Corinthians 1.23—2.4).

Though these things may have discouraged him, he doesn't respond by being irritable and, as a result, damaging relationships and hindering the progress of the gospel. He uses these things as the background against which he responds with positive and enlightening truth.

He deals with their narrow party spirit by helping them to see the broad picture: 'So let no one boast about human leaders. For all things are yours, whether Paul or Apollos or Cephas or the world or life or death or the present or the future – all belong to you, and you belong to Christ, and Christ belongs to God' (1 Corinthians 3.21–23). He responds to their strictures on authority and integrity by reminding them of the twin purpose of his ministry, namely their salvation and the glory of God: 'Yes, everything is for your sake, so that grace, as it extends to more and more people, may increase thanksgiving, to the glory of God' (2 Corinthians 4.15). Paul clearly practised what he preached.

'Love is not irritable'. That doesn't mean that people or things will not get on our nerves – we will be in heaven before that happens! But it does mean that we will not react so negatively to irritation that we damage human relationships and hinder the work of God. Given the inner resources we have in Christ, we need to discover how to use the source of irritation as a background against which we can respond with sensitivity, love and generosity.

Learning to forget

It is generosity that lies at the root of Paul's third and final example of generous contentment in the face of life's trials. 'Love is not resentful', or as the New International Version has it, 'Love keeps no record of wrongs'.

Here again we have an astonishing claim: a description of good practice that cuts across and undermines much of the meanness that poisons human relationships. The harbouring of resentment over past wrongs is one of the major causes of breakdown within families, communities and nations. The decades of sectarian division in Ireland, for instance, have been fuelled by ritualistic recollections of past events, and the bitter resentment that flows from them. The disintegration of families is so often caused by people nursing resentment over past disputes rather than seeking reconciliation. It would be laughable if it wasn't true, but I have known two villages refuse to worship in the same church building because, centuries ago, they were on opposite sides in the Civil War!

Resentment is a cancer which, if it is allowed to grow, will rob us of joy and peace and unhelpfully spill over into the lives of other innocent people. I have known some who can't sleep because of feelings of resentment. They wake up in the night and spend time composing and delivering verbal counter-attacks on those who have wronged them. I meet scores of people who claim that they would be regular churchgoers if only the vicar or a member of the congregation hadn't offended them ten years ago!

I know, of course, that there are some people who just love to be offended, and seem happier when they have found a reason to be so! But when resentment takes over, we do our health and our happiness no favours. When Paul says, 'Love is not resentful', he is outlining a principle that goes to the very heart of the Christian gospel.

It is generally agreed that the word translated 'resentful' comes from the world of accountancy, hence the New International Version translation, 'keeps no score of wrongs'. In other words, love doesn't have a little black book in which it takes note of every evil thing that people do, and holds it against them. It doesn't tally up evil with a view to repaying it with interest. That is very far removed from the gospel of God who, in Christ, Paul tells us, 'was reconciling the world to himself, not counting their trespasses against them, and entrusting the message of reconciliation to us' (2 Corinthians 5.19).

This action of God in Christ conveys the true content of the love that is not resentful. It doesn't store up information about evil and make plans for getting even. That is a recipe for perpetuating evil and is contrary to the way of Christ. Through the cross Jesus Christ took evil upon himself, exposed it for what it was, and disposed of it. How often have you heard people say, regarding a person who has done them wrong, 'I will forgive, but I can never forget'? Given the circumstances, their reaction, if not ideal, may be entirely understandable. But it is still not the way of Christ. He, following the example of his Father, forgave *and* forgot: 'I will forgive their iniquity, and remember their sins no more' (Jeremiah 31.34).

Being human, our willingness to forgive may not always be matched by an ability to forget, or at least not to remember. Memories can be notoriously unpredictable. Nevertheless, if we have the desire to reveal the love that is not resentful, there is every reason to believe that God will heal our memories. Thus, with the help of God, we may be able to overcome destructive self-interest, irritability and resentment, and experience that generous contentment that comes from dependence upon the indwelling Christ.

5

Properly focused

Love does not rejoice in wrongdoing;
but rejoices in the truth.

St Paul was never a half-hearted person. Before his conversion, he was completely focused on the worthy task of safeguarding his religious tradition, following, to the letter, the law of the God of Israel. He saw the emergence of the so-called new religious movement founded by Jesus as a threat to the purity of his traditional religion, and was totally committed to destroying it. As we noted in the Introduction, it was while zealously pursuing the followers of Jesus, in order to throw them into prison, that he dramatically discovered that he had been getting things drastically out of perspective for years. As he persecuted the followers of Jesus in the name of his God, he was brought face to face with the awful truth that it was his God that he had been persecuting. Inadvertently, he had been busy not preparing but destroying the Way of God (Acts 9.1–9).

Clearly, he was devastated at the realization that what he thought was error was, in reality, truth. He was soon to recognize that what he had dismissed as the new Jesus movement was neither new nor a movement, but the promised fulfilment and true expression of the faith of Israel. Jesus was Israel's promised Messiah, the incarnate Son of God, the one who would not only claim to be the Truth, but also make the truth of God visible to us. His encounter with the living Jesus resulted in his focus being radically altered, and even more sharply defined.

It was entirely in keeping with his personality, therefore, that when he wrote to this exciting, gifted and complex community in Corinth, he declared himself to be completely and properly focused. 'When I came to you, brothers and sisters, I did not come proclaiming the mystery of God to you in lofty words or wisdom. For I decided to know nothing among you except Jesus Christ, and him crucified' (1 Corinthians 2.1–2). Given his record of wrongdoing in persecuting the Christian Church, together with his joyful discovery of the truth of God in Jesus Christ, it is not surprising that his song of love encourages Christians to fix their sights not on wrongdoing but on truth. 'Love does not rejoice in wrongdoing; but rejoices in the truth.'

Dubious pleasure

Paul took no pleasure in the recollection of what he had done in persecuting the Church of God and, in this connection, referred to himself as 'the foremost' of sinners (1 Timothy 1.15). But he rejoiced in the amazing mercy and grace of God that could forgive and save a sinner such as he. He didn't get bogged down in distressing memories regarding the past, for Christ had redeemed all of him, including his memories. He had learned to forget painful aspects of the past by concentrating on the pursuit of the prize of God contained in Christ: 'this one thing I do: forgetting what lies behind and straining forward to what lies ahead, I press on towards the goal for the prize of the heavenly call of God in Christ Jesus' (Philippians 3.13–14).

His redeemed focus on the positive aspects of his new life in Christ helps us to understand the significance of his words, 'Love does not rejoice in wrongdoing, but rejoices in the truth.' The converted Paul wasn't 'hung up' on his past wrongdoing but, when he did mention it, it was always for the purpose of drawing attention to the goodness and grace of God. So, as he composes his song of love, he encourages his readers to be similarly focused. They are not to indulge in the dubious pleasure occasioned by other people's wrongdoing, but to find joy in the truth, especially in the truth as found in Jesus Christ.

The suggestion that some people, including Christian people, take pleasure in the wrongdoings of others may seem rather implausible, but it is not. In this regard, I doubt if any other words from Paul's letters have a more up-to-date application than these. Even the most objective view of today's print and broadcast media will bear this out. It seems crammed with lurid detail of other people's misfortunes. Stories of the 'bad and the ugly' appear vastly to outnumber stories of the 'good'. To be fair, the media, often quite properly, shine a spotlight on disasters and the evil deeds that others commit, and in doing so help us to get at an important, if unpalatable, truth. However, the intrusive nature and extended coverage of some of the stories frequently appears to be geared towards titillating the minds and stimulating the imagination of the readers.

It would be easy at this point to blame it all on 'a sensation-seeking' media, as though it alone was responsible for constantly bombarding us with 'bad news'. But that would be unfair and rather short-sighted. Our newspapers sell in vast quantities because the population eagerly buys them and complains if they are not available. Audience ratings, which reveal the level of public interest, largely determine what appears on our television screens. So, clearly, there is something in us to which the coverage of the 'bad and the ugly' appeals. This may not be a very flattering image, but it certainly emphasizes one of the peculiar traits of human nature – very often we seem to prefer to learn about the misfortunes rather than the good fortunes of others.

Questionable practice

It is one thing to learn of their misfortunes, but quite another to look for and rejoice in them. And Paul, as he writes to Christian people, feels constrained to remind them that love does not behave in this way. It doesn't go out of its way to find fault and then rejoice in it. It doesn't insist on digging up the perceived misdemeanours of others and delighting in them. It doesn't waste its time highlighting the bad and the ugly while ignoring the good. There are indications that the Christian congregation in Corinth may not have been free from such perversions of love, and many churches today have more than their share of it!

Douglas, for instance, was a case in point. He could have been a power for good; instead he became an influence for evil. Energetic, intelligent and articulate, he should have been a welcome member of any congregation, a valued addition to any community. Sadly, he became a disruptive element wherever he went, and often destroyed the cohesion and confidence of the small fellowship groups to which he belonged. He took pleasure in the faults and failings of others. Whenever people were invited to exercise leadership in his local church, he would try to undermine their position by spreading poisonous innuendoes about things that had gone wrong in their past. Frequently, as his local church grew in numbers and zeal, he would impute false motives to people, and publicly humiliate them by saying things like, 'Of course, you are well known for pushing yourself forward,' or 'Given your past record, do you think you should be a leader in the church?'

Douglas was a one-man disaster area. He didn't just occasionally behave like a bull in a china shop; he took the china shop with him wherever he went! The results were often devastating, and the more damaging they became, the more pleasure he seemed to get out of it. He finally left the church, despite the gracious love and patience of others towards him, and became a bitter, disillusioned and friendless old man.

He may appear to be an extreme example of wrongful rejoicing, but he is by no means an isolated case. Most of us are aware of those within our acquaintance whose eyes light up at the prospect of a 'good gossip' about the misdemeanours and misfortunes of others. At times, in my work as a Christian minister, I have been shocked at the amount of malice shown by those who should have known better than rejoice at the downfall of a colleague. And, as a senior church leader, investigating situations of pastoral breakdown, I have been surprised at the readiness of some, purely on the basis of rumour, to take pleasure in believing the worst about others. Perhaps I shouldn't have been surprised, for Confucius is alleged to have said, 'There is no greater pleasure than to behold an old friend fall from a rooftop.' It sounds a little perverse until, perhaps, we recognize echoes of it within ourselves. There is a certain delight we all experience when someone exalted is brought low, when, to change the metaphor, those who have been placed, or placed themselves, on a pedestal are forced to come down to earth where, we may be quick to remind them, they belong.

A *subtle variation*

But there may be a more sophisticated form of rejoicing in wrongdoing that we have failed to recognize or been willing to admit. We catch just a glimpse of it in the story told by Jesus of two men who went up into the Temple to pray, one a Pharisee and the other a tax-collector (Luke 18.9–14). The latter had such a sense of his own unworthiness that he couldn't, as it were, look God in the face. Instead, he kept his distance and with bowed head muttered, 'God, be merciful to me, a sinner!' The Pharisee, however, had no difficulty about coming into the presence of God, and did so in a spirit of self-congratulation. 'God, I thank you that I am not like other people: thieves, rogues, adulterers, or even like this tax-collector. I fast twice a week; I give a tenth of all my income.' At the conclusion of the story, Jesus left us in no doubt as to who had the greater integrity and was more acceptable to God. The Pharisee might have gone home feeling more important, but the tax-collector went home forgiven.

Though the story was directed at the specific social and religious attitude prevailing at the time, it adds a pertinence to Paul's conviction that love does not rejoice in wrongdoing. His words were directed at the prevailing situation in Corinth, and through them he was stressing that love takes no self-righteous pleasure in being censorious about the faults of others. Unlike some extremists in the Church, love does not behave like an inquisitor, actively investigating and uncovering what it perceives to be wrong in other people. Unlike the Pharisee, love does not seek to establish its own identity and superiority by shamefully disparaging someone else by way of comparison. That smacks of the blame culture which pervades much of our society, and which looks for scapegoats on which to focus its discontent in order to preserve its own sense of superiority.

Such behaviour, whether in the Church or in society, not only lacks integrity but also reveals a rather sad absence of love.

A powerful combination

There is nothing sad, however, about the presence of truth. On the contrary, says Paul, 'Love rejoices in the truth'. Striving to find fault was not a priority with him. He preferred to affirm and take pleasure in what was commendable and true. Writing to the Philippians, for instance, he urges them to focus their thoughts on those things that would warm their hearts and unify their community. 'If then there is any encouragement in Christ, any consolation from love, any sharing in the Spirit, any compassion and sympathy, make my joy complete: be of the same mind, having the same love, being in full accord and of one mind' (Philippians 2.1–2). Paul was convinced that joy and rejoicing came from concentrating on things that were good and true, and that love was the driving force behind such single-mindedness.

He was right. Too many people have tunnel vision. They become so absorbed by what they see as faults in others that they are blind to the clear evidence of the good things in their lives. I recall a young theological student coming to see me after he had paid a pastoral visit to a leading lay worker in the parish. Much to my surprise he was very agitated, and bordered on the apoplectic as he poured out words of scorn about the man he had just visited. 'Did you know that he's a bookmaker, and if you did what are you going to do about it?'

I remained relatively calm, and took my time before replying: I did know, and was doing exactly the same thing for him as I did for any other parishioner who was looking for support in their daily life and Christian discipleship. In the case of our friend the 'bookie', that meant regularly supplying him with a list of disabled folk who had expressed a wish to be brought to the morning service each week in his specially adapted people-carrier. It meant supporting him and his wife as they spearheaded an aid project in Romania and with the help of many in the congregation and local community regularly sent a van-load of basic supplies to needy refugees in that country.

I spared my colleague further blushes by not mentioning several other aspects of the man's work for the kingdom of God, especially in connection with the disadvantaged. His commitment to these things was undoubtedly motivated by love, and left me and others convinced that we were witnessing, in him, the fruits of the Spirit. Of course, there were issues to be discussed about our friend's 'profession', and he often agonized over them in my presence. But I felt sad that in my colleague's mind a conventional religious 'taboo' was being allowed to blot out so much that was good and true in the bookmaker's life, over which love could rejoice. Once again some words from F. W. Faber's memorable hymn came to mind:

> But we make his love too narrow
> By false limits of our own;
> And we magnify his strictness
> With a zeal he will not own.

A *biblical balance*

The combination of love and truth is crucial for the life and witness of the Church in every age and in all circumstances. They belong together and we must be careful never to play one off against the other.

Some people are convinced that as long we love one another questions of belief and behaviour are of secondary importance. First things first, they say. Put love first and everything else will fall into place, or, as the Beatles sang, 'All you need is love – love is all you need'. That is true, as far as it goes, but the problem is that in biblical terms it doesn't go far enough. Love rejoices in truth, but if the truth is denied or ignored, love cannot rejoice. Love cannot be heedless of moral considerations. For instance, were the two Christian people who left their marriage partners and their young families, convinced that they were on a spiritual journey and their love for one another was all that mattered, absolutely right or tragically misguided? The devastation that followed, especially in the lives of their children, would seem to supply the answer.

Other people are equally convinced that truth comes first, and if we are clear about that everything else will follow. If only it were as simple as that. Human nature being what it is, however, sometimes the last thing we want to hear is the truth. If we have been adamant about another person's wrongdoing, the discovery that we have been completely wrong and dreadfully unfair comes like a hammer blow. In such circumstances we may find ourselves wishing that it were not so! At another level, we can press what we believe to be the truth with an insensitive severity that is devoid of love and compassion. The young student of theology clearly believed that there was an inconsistency in being a bookmaker and a Christian, and demanded that the matter, and perhaps the man, be sorted out. He discovered that the situation was much more complex than he had imagined. As Paul said to another church assembly, 'The fruit of the light is found in all that is good and right and true' (Ephesians 5.9).

Love and truth must go hand in hand. The love of God, which has been poured into our hearts by the Holy Spirit, cannot rejoice when God's commandments are set aside, and the way of life that he requires from us disregarded. By the same token, the truth must not be presented in a manner that separates it from love. Paul's advice that we are to 'speak the truth in love' (Ephesians 4.15) actually carries the sense of 'living the truth in a loving manner', a biblical balance that was beautifully displayed in the life of Jesus, who was himself the truth (John 14.6), and at the same time the perfect expression of the love of God.

Love rejoices in all that is good and true in the lives of others but, supremely, it rejoices in the truth as it is found in Jesus Christ: a truth that speaks of the power of God's love and grace to put right all that is wrong, not only in the lives of others but also in your life and mine.

6

No giving up

*Love bears all things, believes all things,
hopes all things, endures all things.*

Weddings and Oscar awards ceremonies have one thing in
common. Their reception speeches vary in quality and, by
and large, are an acquired taste. A few are brilliant but
many are banal. Some are interesting and others are
boring. Occasionally they are wonderfully humorous, but
not infrequently they have such an embarrassing cringe
factor that some guests look round for a way of escape
while others look up in hope of divine intervention. From
time to time, however, we hear a speech that is truly
memorable, not for its eloquence or erudition, but for its
pertinence and power. It speaks to the heart. Bob made
that kind of speech at his wedding reception.

He had had a chequered life. Born into a tragic
domestic situation, his early nurture had been disturbed
by moving from one foster home to another before being
adopted at the age of 11. Following his adoption, he
made life difficult for himself and his adoptive parents by

his rebellious behaviour. In his late teens, drugs and drink led to trouble with the law and caused most of his friends to give up on him. During that period he was considered by many people, including some who were at his wedding reception, to be 'a thoroughly bad lot'. That's why they listened to his speech with such rapt attention. They had watched in amazement and admiration as his life changed dramatically in his early thirties. With great discipline and application, he had gained a degree through the Open University and had set up in business.

And now, having just been married to Carole, a local schoolteacher, he was on his feet making a speech. Wisely, he kept it short and to the point, thanking the guests for coming and the bride's parents for welcoming him into their family and making it possible for him to marry such a super girl. In most situations what he said next would have been quite unexceptional, but given his background it was immensely moving. 'Finally', he said, 'I want to thank my own parents for their patience and resilience. There was no limit to their love. They never gave up on me.'

Bob's punchline was powerful. It could have been written by St Paul, who made a similar point when he wrote: 'Love bears all things, believes all things, hopes all things, endures all things.' Though he didn't put these words from his song to music, they nevertheless form a four-part harmony on the theme, 'Love never gives up'.

Compassionate realism

In saying that love 'bears all things', Paul isn't describing godly resignation in the face of undeserved suffering, but a down-to-earth reaction in the face of life's realities.

There is almost the suggestion that love is 'streetwise' and capable of coping with anything life throws at it. As one version puts it, 'There is nothing love cannot face' (REB). The Greek verb 'to bear' means 'to cover' or 'protect'. It suggests that love does not go around exposing or publicizing other people's faults and mistakes. Instead, it draws a veil over them, and although the verb is different a similar thought is contained in the familiar saying, 'Love covers a multitude of sins' (1 Peter 4.8).

Such reaction on the part of love shows a compassionate understanding of the realities of life. It is not surprised by what it discovers about life. It reveals an awareness of human frailties and makes appropriate allowances for them. The psalmist suggests that this is also the way God's mind works. God doesn't keep a tally of our human failings – if he did, there would be no hope for any of us: 'If you, O LORD, should mark iniquities, Lord, who could stand?' (Psalm 130.3). He bears with us, quick to understand our human weaknesses, and ready to forgive and support us through all the vicissitudes of life.

Most of us are grateful for those family members and friends who relate to us in a similar way. They know our faults and foibles but they don't keep reminding us of them. They bear them, in the sense that they put them out of sight and out of mind, and get on with the business of loving and supporting us. Such a godly attitude is in deep contrast to those moments of acute embarrassment when an acquaintance insists on washing their dirty linen in public, telling the world of the shortcomings of their partner and, by the same token, exposing their own!

Love does not behave in this way. It bears all things. It covers and protects those it loves. It doesn't turn a blind eye to their failings and mistakes, but it refuses to drag them into the public domain, preferring, instead, to cover them with silence in the name of love. Bob's adoptive parents were just as aware of his shortcomings as those friends who gave up on him, but their love was stronger than the disappointments and heartaches they bore on his account.

We see a classic, if stark, example of this in the way Jesus related to Judas Iscariot. He knew that Judas was a complex character, full of zeal on the one hand and intrigue on the other. He had known for some time of Judas' decision to betray him. But, rather than expose him, even at the Last Supper, Jesus offered him a sign of friendship, sharing the bread with him before Judas went off to bargain for Jesus' capture (Luke 22.14–23). And, though he knew the die was cast, Jesus still didn't give up on Judas, but as he left the Garden of Gethsemane accepted his kiss of love and friendship knowing it was also the sign of betrayal (Mark 14.43–46). Love bears all things, even betrayal.

Persistent faith

Love behaves in this way because it never loses faith: 'Love believes all things'. That doesn't mean love is gullible and will believe anything. But it does mean that love will not jump to false conclusions or be hasty in forming negative judgements about people and things.

Disappointed by his adolescent rebelliousness, some of Bob's friends 'wrote him off' prematurely. His adoptive parents, however, aware of the traumatic circumstances of his early years, gave him the benefit of the doubt, and preferred to keep looking and waiting to see the best in him, rather than settle for the worst. Their love was constant because their faith was persistent. It had a dogged quality that held firm in good times and in bad. Love never gave up because it never lost faith. It was always ready to believe the best.

I sometimes wonder what would have happened to the Church of Jesus Christ if he had not dealt with his first disciples in this gracious way. He saw the best in Peter, for instance, long before Peter saw it in himself. He kept believing in him, even when Peter made life difficult for him. When most of us would have written him off for his cowardly denials in the shadow of the cross, Jesus, after his resurrection, restored, renewed and re-commissioned Peter to fulfil the purpose for which he had first been chosen (John 21.15–19). He never lost faith in Peter.

And he did the same for Thomas, who was missing when the risen Jesus came to his disciples on that first Easter evening. Later, when they told him about it, he was quite belligerent in expressing his unbelief, declaring that he wouldn't believe until he had probed the wounds of Jesus for proof. There are some in today's Church who would have believed the worst about Thomas, declaring him unfit to be an apostle. But not Jesus. He came back for Thomas, and even offered his wounds for inspection and probing fingers. False love would have believed the worst and 'dropped' Thomas from the team. True love kept faith and enriched the history of the Church by including him.

Many of us will thank God that, as young Christians, there were those who had the love to believe all things and to see things in us that we couldn't see in ourselves. They kept faith with us until we reached maturity and fulfilled our potential. And some, like myself, who have felt privileged, and terrified, to be called to leadership in the Church of God, are eternally grateful to those who understood the demanding nature of the task and supported us in it. They appreciated the fact that leadership necessitated being on frontiers of mission, with all the risks of being misunderstood and misrepresented, and they kept faith with us and with love, believing all things, including our commitment and integrity.

Paul's conviction that love believes all things is a vital reminder to the Church that our life is based on trust, our trust in God and our trust in each other as children of God. His readiness to keep faith with us, despite our shortcomings, provides the template for our attitude to others. Love is not gullible but generous. It never ceases to believe all things.

More than optimism

And, as the third line of Paul's four-part harmony makes clear, love never ceases to hope. 'Love hopes all things'. This doesn't mean that love is eternally optimistic. God does not offer us unreasoning optimism; he provides hope. And hope does not ignore reality; it takes careful note of it, and puts it in perspective. When Paul wrote about hope, he didn't ignore the reality of the broken and suffering world all around him. He took it fully into account and placed it in the larger context of the glory that was to come. Indeed, he saw the present sufferings as the birth pangs of a new creation, when creation would be 'set free from its bondage to decay and will obtain the freedom of the glory of the children of God' (Romans 8.21). It wasn't that Paul wore rose-coloured spectacles, or assumed that it would be 'all right on the night'. His was a sure and certain hope, anchored in the love and grace of God, and based on his own experience of the risen Christ, in whom failure is never final and through whom love always triumphs. 'I am convinced', he declared, 'that nothing will be able to separate us from the love of God in Christ' (Romans 8.18–39).

Bob's parents would not have been able to quote Paul, chapter and verse, but they had the same conviction about hope. It never gives up. And while at times their faith may have wavered, their hope held firm and was eventually realized.

Once again, the attitude of Jesus provides us with practical wisdom. He never viewed people as hopeless. When society rejected them, he rescued them. He not only healed the lame and the blind, he also gave them dignity and purpose. Prostitutes and adulterers were befriended, forgiven and restored. He held hope for the hopeless.

I saw a beautiful example of this while on a pastoral walk through an inner-city parish. En route I visited a care centre for children with severe learning difficulties. There was a limited number of children but each had a qualified carer to look after them, and as I watched their compassionate care I was overwhelmed by the feeling that I was 'on holy ground'. One memory stands out. A little boy, possibly four or five years old, lay on a bed unable to move anything but his head, and then only a few inches to left or right. However, he was provided with a special pillow, and when he turned his head to the left, the movement triggered the playing of gentle music. He was slowly learning how to trigger and enjoy the music, and on the day I visited he was smiling, and his carer was thrilled, because he had got the hang of it. To some it might not have seemed much of an achievement, but his carer assured me that it was a massive step forward and a source of great encouragement to her, and to the boy's parents. I asked her how she coped with such a demanding task day in and day out. Quietly she replied, 'Together with his parents, I hold hope for him.'

It was a moving and profound comment which, I believe, provides a unique insight into the meaning of 'love hopes all things'. These words, as we have seen, encourage us not to despair of people and things, because our hope is in God, and with him failure does not have the last word; hope never gives up. But there are situations where the future seems so bleak that there is not even a glimmer of hope. There are people who, because of the circumstances surrounding them, seem to find hope impossible. It is then, when they can't hold hope for themselves, that we must hold hope for them, in the name of the God who is the source of the love that 'hopes all things'.

Purposeful perseverance

Paul completes his four-part harmony with the assurance that 'love endures all things'. In the face of hardship, discouragement or rejection, love doesn't grind its teeth and complain, 'Why me, what have I done to deserve this?' The Greek verb 'to endure' conveys a much more positive note. Far from suggesting a reluctant acceptance of the inevitable, it implies confidence and courage in the face of difficulty. Love sees difficulties in positive rather than in negative terms. It perseveres with a purpose, for it knows that trials, of whatever kind, are the raw materials that help our growth towards maturity in Christ.

To be honest, it doesn't always feel like this and, for the sake of others, we need to be a little careful lest our words give a false impression of our true feelings. Love endures all things, but it doesn't pretend always to enjoy it. If I waken at three o'clock in the morning with raging toothache, I don't invite my wife to get up and join me in singing the doxology! If we are insincerely, and insensitively triumphalist in the face of our hardships, we may discourage others who are anxiously, and perhaps unsuccessfully, struggling with theirs.

And there is another facet of 'enduring' that we need to be brutally honest about, namely self-inflicted hardship or difficulty caused by our own foolishness and pride. If we have been unfair, unkind or unprofessional in our relationships with others and, as a result, they give us a hard time, we must be careful to get things in perspective. They may not be making life difficult for us because we are Christians, but because we have acted improperly. In such circumstances, love's priority might be that we repent rather than endure.

Despite these things, endurance, of the kind that springs from love, does bring glory to God, encouragement to others and lasting benefits to us. It brings glory to God, for his love is the source of it. It brings encouragement to others because it reveals that positive, purposeful perseverance is possible in the face of adversity. It brings benefits to us because it not only deepens our trust in God but also enables us to reveal something of the fruits of the spirit and the character of Jesus Christ.

Love's endurance was seen to perfection in him. He didn't welcome adversity but he endured it in the proper frame of mind. He didn't resent it, or compromise his principles in order to avoid it; indeed, he warned his followers to expect it, and taught them to face it with realism and confidence: 'In the world you face persecution. But take courage; I have conquered the world!' (John 16.33).

But Jesus didn't just speak words of wisdom about endurance; he made them visible in his own life. He wasn't bitter about the misunderstanding, mis-representation and violent intrigue that dogged his footsteps in the closing months of his life and work on earth. He was realistic. He saw it for what it was – the natural opposition of darkness to light, of evil to goodness. He was confident in the purposes of God his Father. He wasn't, as it were, dragged kicking and screaming to the cross. He faced it with courage and fortitude, declaring, 'No one takes my life from me, but I lay it down of my own accord' (John 10.18). Like an athlete who runs with determination and joyful anticipation of winning the prize, he was 'the pioneer and perfecter of our faith, who for the sake of the joy that was set before him endured the cross, disregarding its shame, and has taken his seat at the right hand of the throne of God' (Hebrews 12.1–2).

The love that enabled him to persevere against all the odds is the same love which bids us to 'endure all things'. His Father's response in raising him to life and exalting him to glory should give us confidence to do just that, always remembering that our Lord's confidence was accompanied by realism, humility and trust.

7

Here to stay

Love never ends.
But as for prophecies, they will come to an end;
as for tongues, they will cease;
as for knowledge, it will come to an end.

Sunday mornings were always a bit special in my childhood home and memories of them remain vivid. My father rarely went to church, but gave his children every encouragement to attend the large Sunday school that was attached to our local parish church. A practical feature of that encouragement was to supply each of us with money to put in the collection bag. That wasn't as simple as it first seems, though undoubtedly more generous, for we were large in number and formed an expectant queue in the front room of our small house each Sunday morning. He always began the distribution with the eldest, and since I was the youngest I was always fearful that there would be nothing left by the time he reached me. However, I was never disappointed.

But the thing I remember most was his huge smile and dramatic action as he completed his weekly handout. With a broad grin, he would reach both hands into his pockets and, pulling out to full stretch the lining from each, would say, 'All gone.' He had nothing more to give. His pockets were empty. His cash had come to an end.

A *permanent supply*

I cannot read verse 8 of Paul's song or hymn of love without recalling this childhood memory, with its simple illustration of the transitory nature of human resources, in contrast to the permanence of the love that has its source in God. Unlike my earthly father, my heavenly Father doesn't say of his resources, 'All gone! Here today and gone this morning', but, 'Love never ends'. There is always more. It is here to stay.

It is this fundamental truth that marks a turning point, and important shift of emphasis, in the song of love. We focused on the necessity of love (13.1–3) in Chapter 1, and reflected on the nature and work of love (13.4–7) in the following five chapters. But now the song changes into a slightly different key, as it were. The overall theme remains the same, but there is a new approach that puts our past, present and future life into perspective, as Paul speaks about the permanence of love (13.8–13). He is convinced that love will still be around when the things on which we humans so often depend, and in which we frequently take pride, will be gone for good, with no hope, or need, of their return. He believes that love is unconquerable, having an enduring quality that will survive every attempt to crush it. It will never end.

We are given a beautiful, poetic preview of this in some well-known words from the Old Testament: 'Many waters cannot quench love, neither can floods drown it' (Song of Songs 8.7). Like many books of poems, the Song of Songs is not always easy to read, though unquestionably its central topic is love. The difficulty is that we are not always sure whether it is God's love or human love that is being spoken about, though the answer, almost certainly, is both.

To some extent, that is also true of Paul's song of love. When the word love is used, it is not entirely clear whether we are to think in terms of human love or the love of God. Sometimes, in our theological discussions, the distinction may be drawn too sharply.

Of course, there is a clear sense in which love is human, since most of us practise it every day, but the source from which that love emanates is divine. The love that exists between the three persons of the Holy Trinity – Father, Son, and Holy Spirit – is the source from which all love springs. Nevertheless, despite its divine source, human love is subject to the frailties of our human nature, and at times is found wanting. Obviously that was happening in the church at Corinth, and was one of the reasons why Paul included this song of love in his first letter to that church.

God's love, on the other hand, is perfect. It is neither partial nor prejudiced. It is not conditional. It is offered in its fullness to friend and foe alike. This contrast between the perfection of God's love and the frailty of our own is beautifully expressed in William Cowper's famous hymn, 'Hark my soul'. The hymn is really a dialogue between God and the human soul, and two of its verses sum up the point I have been trying to make:

> Mine is an unchanging love,
> higher than the heights above,
> deeper than the depths beneath,
> free and faithful, strong as death.

Lord, it is my chief complaint,
that my love is weak and faint:
yet I love thee and adore;
O for grace to love thee more!

A strange encouragement

Strange as it may seem, I find the occasional uncertainty, as to whether or not Paul is speaking about human love or the love of God, remarkably encouraging. The fact that it is not always easy to differentiate between them suggests a close connection that is full of creative possibilities.

'Love never ends', writes Paul. In other words, it never fails, or, according to the Greek verb, never falls, something that is not always true of human love, which often falls short of the ideal Paul outlines when he writes of how love acts and what love avoids (13.4–7). It is important to note that he is not dangling before us an impossible dream that, because of our human frailty, will end in failure and produce feelings of guilt. Rather, he is encouraging us to aim high, to set our aspirations on the more excellent way.

In this connection we have already noticed that love is one of the fruits of the Spirit (Galatians 5.22), and that 'God's love has been poured into our hearts through the Holy Spirit that has been given to us' (Romans 5.5). This means that we are adequately resourced to aim for the ideal in our love for God and in our love for others. Indeed, we are to reveal that we belong to Christ by the love we bear towards one another (John 13.35).

Nevertheless, as Cowper's hymn reminds us, our love, despite the infinite resource available to it, is often 'weak and faint'. When, for instance, we react to criticism with a verbal belligerence that goes beyond self-defence and seeks to humiliate another, that is not the response of love. Similarly, when we exalt ourselves at the expense of someone else, that is not an attitude of love, just as the forming of judgements about another, on the basis of hearsay and gossip, is a denial of love. Failures of love in these and other ways prevent us from measuring up to Paul's ideal of love, but the grace of God and the Spirit of God bring us encouragement in our desire to do so.

The Scriptures teach that the grace of God is not only ready to forgive our failures of love, but is also able to strengthen and help us to get it right next time. It is through grace that the Spirit pours the love of God into our hearts in the first place, so clearly he wants us to get it right. Our problem may be in admitting that we got it wrong, and that our reaction to a particular person was not a reflection of our love for God or for them, but an indication that we still had some way to go in our pursuit of the ideal. Once we have admitted and repented of our attitude, however, the way is open for us to be renewed in love, by God's Spirit, and to receive a fresh supply of grace to empower us to get closer to God's ideal. We are not left to our own devices in this matter. God is on our side.

A second cause for encouragement is the fact that God desires to reveal his love through us. He wants us to be his agents of love within the community in which we are set.

I saw this, to a remarkable degree, in the life of Rachel, who lived with her husband in a small country parish. They had no family, and most of their time was given to serving others within the local community. Rachel was particularly gifted in this way. She quite simply loved people, and nothing was too much trouble if it would help someone else. She visited the sick, comforted the bereaved, and wrote little notes of encouragement to those going through hard times. She never gossiped, spoke harsh words, or complained about other people. Far from being a 'goodie-goodie', however, she was intensely human, with a wonderful sense of humour. People loved her company. Young and old saw her as a friend and, often, a confidant. She made the love of God visible in her community.

The most remarkable aspect of this true story, however, came when Rachel's husband died rather suddenly. At that point the entire village became a visible expression of the love of God towards her. Immense kindness, understanding and sensitive pastoral care was quietly and unobtrusively extended to her. It was very moving and, on reflection, incredibly exciting and humbling. God's love was seen in Rachel's love for others. And, having seen that love, the community's response to her need enabled God's love to be seen in them. It was an amazing twin-example of the truth recorded by Dr John Stott, that 'God who is love still loves, and today his love is seen in our love.'

A glimpse of eternity

The fact that God's love may be seen in our love is not only exciting, and rather humbling; it also provides us with a further, perhaps unexpected, insight into the words, 'Love never ends'. We know, of course, that since all love has its source in God, and he is eternal, so also is love. Like God, it is not limited to time and, therefore, will never end. Some may wish to relegate such an insight to the realm of impractical theory. But I believe we catch a glimpse of its practical truth in the story of Rachel and her village community. God's love, which existed from all eternity, was made present and visible in her, today. But the love of God, shown in and through her love, prompted a response that revealed the love of God in and through the love of her village community. There was a kind of chain reaction; love produced love. And, if I may put it this way, as long as God lives and loves, and continues to allow his love to be seen in our love, then we share in, and help to tell, the eternal story of the love that never comes to an end.

But, unlike my father's dramatic conclusion to his Sunday morning handout, there is more!

Love is not just the language of earth; it is the language of heaven and the kingdom of God. The love that we currently share with God and with others is a foretaste of the age to come. It is an indication that, through the death and resurrection of Jesus Christ, the age to come, to a limited degree, has already arrived, and we can look with expectation to the fullness of its coming in the kingdom. Our life of love on earth is a preparation for our life in that kingdom of love, in the eternal presence of the God of love.

This is not mere pious rhetoric; it forms the background to the change of key in the song, which began with Paul's words, 'Love never ends'. They mark the beginning of a passage in which thoughts of the 'end time' are very much in Paul's mind. The time when the kingdom of God would come on earth as in heaven underlines everything he says in the closing verses of his song, and none more so than here in verse 8.

Paul returns to where he began, to the contrast between love and spiritual gifts (13.1–7), only this time the emphasis is on the enduring quality of love. It is against the background of love's permanence that Paul sets the transient gifts on which the Corinthians placed such importance and in which they took such pride. The result is a devastating assessment, in which those things that seem so crucial to the life of the Church on earth will become redundant in the fullness of life in the kingdom of God.

In three short sentences, he refers to these things in the light of eternity. 'Prophecies, they will come to an end'. They will cease. They will be done away with, for they will no longer be needed. There will be no need for people to tell us what God is saying. He will tell us himself, as we stand in his presence. 'As for tongues, they will cease'. They will lie still. There will be no need for any special communication from God in a language that needs interpretation. God will speak clearly to us and we will understand. 'As for knowledge, it will come to an end'. Knowledge, or the understanding of mysteries, will no longer be the preserve of the few. All of us will know everything that God wants us to know.

Prophecy, tongues and knowledge have their place, and it is an important place, in the life of the church in Corinth, or anywhere else. That place, however, is both limited and temporary. These things belong to the Church on earth, and they will pass away. Love, however, spans both earth and heaven, and is the language of God, which all can understand and none can be without. It is reassuring to know, therefore, that 'love never ends'. It is here to stay.

8

Partial and complete

For we know only in part,
and we prophesy only in part;
but when the complete comes,
the partial will come to an end.

One of the more common criticisms levelled at preachers is that they don't always know when to stop. Some appear to be timing their sermons by a calendar rather than a clock. Others preach as though there was no tomorrow, and try to get as much as possible in today. As a young lay preacher, using brief notes rather than a script, the problem was not knowing *when* to stop, but knowing *how* to stop. Like a gramophone needle that was stuck, there was a tendency to be repetitive. And, like coming across a large and unfamiliar roundabout, I went round more than once before I found the right exit. At the time I consoled, or perhaps fooled, myself that such repetitiveness was caused by nervousness rather than incompetence.

Paul needed no such excuse, though some feel that the closing section of his song of love (13.8–13) is somewhat repetitive. It is true, he seems to be making the same point, in a variety of ways and with the help of different illustrations, but that is the sign of a good teacher, especially since the point he is getting across so graphically is vital to his argument. Having made that point in verse 8, he re-emphasizes it in a different way in each of the verses that follow. His underlying theme is still the supremacy of love, but he is intent that it should be seen in the larger context of the age that is to come. In other words, he is linking earth and heaven – which, come to think of it, is a worthy aim for every preacher of the gospel of God.

It's a long story

Those who have had the privilege of preaching that gospel for years will be the first to admit the limitations of their knowledge of God. It seems that the more they discover about God, the more they become aware of the vast amount they don't know. This is true not just in the realm of religion and theology, but in so many other professional disciplines. Most of us, for instance, are personally grateful for the significant progress made in the field of medical research. Each generation pushes the boundaries of knowledge and skill further, thus prolonging the lives of thousands. The fact that such research never ceases, and that extremely gifted scientists are continually engaged on the frontiers of knowledge, is an indication that the more they know the more they realize how much they don't know – hence their dedication to the cause of more complete knowledge and understanding.

Paul had begun his song with the devastating assessment that spiritual gifts, without love, were seriously flawed, if not useless. Now, in contrast to the enduring quality of love, he begins to talk of the day when some of those spiritual gifts will fade away. He had spoken of the necessity of love in giving credibility to the gifts of tongues, knowledge and prophecy. He now speaks of the time when, in view of the supremacy of love, these gifts will not be needed; they will be surplus to requirements. He starts to demonstrate this in the skilful way he constructs the final section of his song (13.8–13). Having spoken of tongues, knowledge and prophecy at the beginning (13.1–3), he returns to them in verse 8 in order to give warning of their ultimate demise. But now, as the song moves towards its final crescendo, he drops them one by one – and tongues is the first to disappear.

For the moment he concentrates on knowledge and prophecy: 'For we know only in part, and we prophesy only in part'. If I may put it in everyday language, Paul seems to be suggesting that the story of God is a long story and we don't yet know the half of it. Whatever value the Corinthian Christians placed on knowledge and prophecy, they are reminded that these things are only partial. It is true that they have the nature of special revelations from God, in which he shares mysteries and inner secrets regarding his plans and purposes, but they are by no means the whole story. They convey only a part of it and, almost certainly, a very small part of it.

Not long ago I led a group of Christians on a pilgrimage to the city of Rome. One of the many highlights of the pilgrimage was a visit to the Vatican Museum. Its galleries are numerous, its treasures magnificent, and its policy towards visitors superb, and relatively subtle. As soon as we arrived in the impressive entrance hall, we saw an arrow pointing to the famous Sistine Chapel which, most visitors agree, is the *pièce de résistance* of the tour. However, as we obediently followed a series of similar arrows for the next three hours, we discovered that we were being directed through each of the many galleries, until eventually we reached the Sistine Chapel – it was the last port of call before the exit! With tongue in cheek, one of our party remarked that it was rather like visiting Ikea, in the sense that the layout of that store seems designed to ensure that you pass through every department before you discover the way out.

Though Paul doesn't speak in such terms, I can't help believing that the contrast he draws between our limited knowledge and the fullness of knowledge to be experienced in the immediate presence of God at the end of the age, is like still being in the first gallery, if not the entrance hall, of the Vatican Museum, rather than in the unsurpassable splendour of the Sistine Chapel.

It is a sobering thought. In exercising or receiving the ministry of the spiritual gift of knowledge, we are only grasping fragments of God's mighty story of salvation. We must await the full vision of the God who is love, before we can embrace the fullness of knowledge he will impart to us. As for prophecy, it draws aside only a tiny corner of the veil that covers the plans and purposes of God, giving us merely a glimpse of what might be in store for us in the kingdom of light and love.

Knowledge and prophecy have been, and are, valuable gifts of the Spirit to the life of the Church on earth. Time, however, will show that through their distinctive and estimable ministry, we have still only touched the fringe of the glory of God yet to be revealed. Our knowledge of God and his ways is, at best, partial: 'We know only in part, and we prophesy only in part'.

With a glorious end

But if it is a sobering thought that we are only touching the fringe of the knowledge of God, by the same token it becomes an exhilarating prospect. The story may be long, with lots more to discover, but the end is sure and the story will be complete – the last page won't be missing. There are glorious times ahead for the people of God.

That is the vision held out by Paul, and in keeping with the theme of his song it is centred on love. 'But when the complete comes, the partial will come to an end.' Various Bible versions, in their attempts to get as close as possible to the meaning of this verse, provide us with a choice of words to contrast with the term 'partial', the description given of knowledge and prophecy. So, for instance, we have 'wholeness' (REB), 'perfection' (NIV) and 'complete' (NRSV). Though all have their merits, I am drawn to the thought of completion. It suggests to me 'consummation', which is entirely in keeping with the emphasis on 'the end time', the age to come, that underlies this concluding section of Paul's song of love.

The word 'complete' implies that our partial knowledge of God will be replaced with the whole truth about God. The complete vision of the God who is love will result in other things, though valuable in themselves, being left behind or set aside. In the blazing light and splendour of the love in which is revealed the total truth about God, 'the partial will come to an end'.

Part of our difficulty in understanding and rejoicing at the prospect of all this is caused by the popular meaning attached to the term 'love' in our society. It can refer to anything from affection to desire, devotion to selfishness, erotic behaviour to enjoyment of sport. It often has a highly emotional and sentimental content which, if imposed upon the phrase 'God is love' can seriously distort our view of God, generating a flood of platitude and mawkishness that doesn't do our religious practice any favours. A presentation of the love of God as some kind of sentimental sweetness with a soft centre is a travesty of the truth. God, as love, expresses his being in strong, dynamic and practical ways. Nowhere is this better expressed than in those words, claimed to contain the kernel of the gospel: 'For God so loved the world that he gave his only Son, so that everyone who believes in him may not perish but may have eternal life' (John 3.16).

The phrase 'God is love' (1 John 4.16) is not some kind of sentimental slogan that we produce to bring ourselves and others some reassurance when facing life's uncertainties. It is much more than that. It is not a partial description of God, to which when occasion demands we tack on other things like goodness and grace, justice and judgement. It is much more than that. It is a description of the being and nature of God in his completeness. God is not only the source of love, but love itself. To say 'God is love' doesn't mean that love is one of his many endeavours, but that all his endeavours, all his actions, emerge from his love. All his attributes, including his goodness and grace, his justice and judgement, are related to his essential nature of love. Love and truth belong together in Christian faith and practice, and they are bound together in the being and nature of God. God is love, and the complete truth of God's being is summed up in his love.

Again, this is no grand, high-blown theory totally divorced from realities of everyday life. It has a strong impact on the way we live and relate to other people. The

Greek word *agape*, which Christians adopted to describe the love that has its source in God, has a strong ethical content. It dominates the Bible's teaching regarding the right way God wants us to live in relation to others. The word, in keeping with the being of God, describes the Father's nature (1 John 4.16), the Son's example (John 15.12) and the Spirit's fruit (Galatians 5.22) in terms of love. In doing so, it covers every aspect of human experience, and makes demands upon the quality of our character: 'Love is patient; love is kind' (1 Corinthians 13.4); the way we think: 'Let the same mind be in you that was in Christ Jesus' (Philippians 2.5); and the way we behave: 'Let us love, not in word or speech, but in truth and action' (1 John 3.18). Far from simply being an interesting theory, the reality of which may be discovered in the next world, so to speak, the vision of God, as love, is a strong incentive to formative and practical living in this world.

Spiritual consistency

So, the relationship between this world and the next was an important element in Paul's song. The age to come was very much in his mind, and needs to be in ours, if we are to appreciate the truth of what he is saying. On the surface, it may seem just a little inconsistent that spiritual gifts should first be given, then pronounced to be flawed, unless accompanied by love, and finally declared to be redundant. But, beneath the surface, as we shall see, there is total consistency, due to the ministry of the Holy Spirit, who is active and a prime mover both in the present age and that which is to come.

In his second letter to the Corinthians, when speaking

about the Christian's hope of life after death, Paul reminds them that the Holy Spirit is the pledge or guarantee of the eternal inheritance into which they shall enter fully in the age to come. 'He who has prepared us for this very thing is God, who has given us the Spirit as a guarantee' (2 Corinthians 5.5). In other words, the new creation, made possible through the death and resurrection of Jesus, and promised by God to his people, is anticipated in the down payment of the Spirit that Christians have already received. He is the guarantee or first instalment of that which God has promised. In that sense, with the coming of the Spirit, the age to come has already penetrated this present age.

Among the many things the creative Spirit has brought to this present age are his spiritual gifts, about which Paul has much to say (1 Corinthians 12—14). They are given to God's people for the building up of his Church on earth, and we must learn to use them wisely and well. But the Spirit who gives gifts like knowledge and prophecy to the people of God in the present age is the same Spirit who is the guarantor of the age to come. The gifts are preparatory, given to help prepare the people of God for their ultimate destiny. They are temporary; they were never meant to be anything else. They belong to this particular period of time, when the age to come overlaps the present age. But when the complete comes, when the kingdom of God comes in its fullness, there will be no further need of them. The time of preparation will be over. There will be no need for a partial glimpse, when the completeness of love and truth will be revealed in the glory of God. There is no need for torchlight when the sun has risen.

9

Growing up

When I was a child, I spoke like a child,
I thought like a child, I reasoned like a child;
when I became an adult,
I put an end to childish ways.

Paul was a wise and sensitive pastor. He knew that the contrast he had drawn between the partial and the complete would, initially, upset a few people in the congregation – especially those who had a vested interest in tongues, knowledge or prophecy. The implication that these gifts, given by the Spirit and highly valued, would eventually become unnecessary was a bitter pill to swallow. So Paul, as he did when he spoke with such force about the indispensable gift of love (13.1–3), speaks again in the first person singular. This time, however, he doesn't use devastating images, like noisy gongs and clanging cymbals, to make his point. Instead, he speaks in more gentle tones about human life, and his experience of the journey from childhood to adulthood.

The tone may have been gentle and sensitive, but such was the simplicity, logic and universal application of what he said that it may have been even more incisive than his comments about gongs and cymbals.

It expressed deep truth in everyday human terms and its thrust was inescapable. 'When I was a child, I spoke like a child, I thought like a child, I reasoned like a child; when I became an adult, I put an end to childish ways.' It is an experience common to us all, though some seem reluctant or unable to make the transition.

Infantile attitude

That was certainly true of some among the Corinthian Christians who, in their progress towards spiritual maturity, thought they were in the vanguard but in reality were lagging far behind. The thrust of this seemingly innocent illustration would not have been lost on them, for he had already referred to them as 'infants in Christ' (1 Corinthians 3.1). It was a reference to his first visit when he had brought the message of the gospel to them and, despite early opposition, had stayed for 18 months and won many converts (Acts 18.5–12). After he left them, however, some became proud of their sophisticated grasp of the faith. They saw themselves as 'adults' and dismissed others as mere 'children' who, unlike them, were unable to cope with intellectual strong meat, and had to make do with a gentler diet of milk, as supplied by Paul during his time with them.

Their attitude caused serious division in the church, so Paul had to write and tell them some home truths. He reminded them that in those early days, when they first became Christians, he had fed them with food that was entirely appropriate for those new in the faith. 'When I came to you, brothers and sisters, I did not come proclaiming the mystery of God to you in lofty words or wisdom. For I decided to know nothing among you except Jesus Christ, and him crucified' (1 Corinthians 2.1–2). In other words, he spoke clearly and simply about the person and work of Jesus Christ, which is the core of the gospel and the proper foundation on which to build new faith. New Christians, like new infants, must learn to walk before they run. If that was 'milk', so be it. They weren't ready for anything else.

Paul's devastating appraisal of this sophisticated group, however, was that they still weren't ready for anything else! Their indulgence in personality cults, and their acceptance of disagreeable factions within the church was an indication that their attitude, far from being adult, was childish in the extreme. They had not put an end to childish things. Their knowledge was still like the knowledge of a child. In overvaluing tongues and prophecy, they had undervalued love. Their lives showed little sign of spiritual transition. Cerebral sophistication was no substitute for practical love. The renewal of the mind should lead to practical action towards those around us. In particular, it should prevent us from being proud of ourselves and dismissive of others. It should provoke us to love our neighbour as Christ loved us. Such evidence of growth to maturity was missing.

Childish behaviour

It is no coincidence that Paul's simple illustration of the progress from childhood to adulthood is quoted often across a wide spectrum of literature. It has a timeless pertinence and power that resonates in every age and in many circumstances. Frequently, major problems in the world and in the Church are caused by adults who have not put an end to childish things. There are too many people and groups who behave like spoilt children, demanding attention and stamping their feet or throwing a tantrum if they don't get it.

I remember, as though it were yesterday, a frustrating experience when I was a schoolboy. It causes me to smile now, but then I was really fed up and no doubt sometimes showed childish annoyance. A group of boys of my age were mad about football. We regularly formed scratch teams and played together, morning, noon and night. Education came a poor second to the beautiful game. In time, most of us became sufficiently skilled to play for the school team which won the National Schools' Cup.

But in those early days, one player stood out and, later in life became a well-known star. He was the only one of us who owned a proper leather football, so we were dependent on him if we wanted a proper game. The only problem was that if things didn't go his way, if his side were losing, or if one of us 'upended' him and came away with the ball, he became upset. And when he was upset, he was prone to 'take his ball home', and leave us to finish the game with the help of a tennis ball. 'It's my ball, so it's my game,' was his motto. He was a real pain.

But we mustn't criticize him too much; after all, he was only a child. However, I have lost count of the number of occasions when I have witnessed a similar scenario played out in the church among adults, who had a slightly more refined way of taking their ball home, when things were not to their liking, or they had had a run-in with the vicar. They would indulge in an ecclesiastical version of industrial action. Their planned-giving covenant wouldn't be renewed, for instance, and they would resign from the church committee. If unfamiliar tunes were played to well-known hymns, they wouldn't sing them. Some, with an ostentatious display of humility, would move to sit at the back of the church – behind a pillar if possible! And, lest we should imagine that only lay people play this particular game, there are many ministers who are experts at it – including those who, metaphorically speaking, stamp their feet when they don't get their own way, or use the sermon to get their own back on those who have upset them.

We may hesitate to call these things childish, though they clearly display the behavioural pattern of some children and they certainly indicate that we have not yet reached the spiritual maturity of adulthood for which we, and God, may long. They suggest that in a selfish pursuit of those things we desire, and a corresponding petulance if we don't get them, love may have been forgotten.

Necessary determination

Besides love, another thing that must not be forgotten is the determination that is necessary if we are to make progress towards spiritual maturity. It doesn't happen automatically. It is true that the physical transition from childhood to adulthood takes places naturally, but the implication of Paul's words, 'I put an end to childish ways', suggests that he made a determined effort to ensure that his thinking, speaking and reasoning were no longer that of a child but of a mature adult.

I don't believe for one moment that he was being dismissive of the thought processes of childhood; indeed, the words he uses cannot be interpreted in that way. Thinking, speaking, reasoning, have a strong intellectual content. They imply that children don't simply function at the emotional level, but that they work things out for themselves and have a reason for the activities they pursue and the actions they take. Those of us who are blessed with children and grandchildren have learned the hard way that children can't be fobbed off with dubious arguments. They are remarkably quick to recognize the unreasonableness of some of the things we ask of them, and many are extremely articulate in pointing out the flaws in our attempts at logical persuasion.

So Paul, in referring to children, may be implying that adults should show a similar determination in working things out for themselves, and to come to the proper conclusion that their adult status requires mature words, thoughts, decisions and behaviour. The strength of his conviction in this matter is marked by his choice of verb. He is determined not to be governed by childish attitudes, but to have done with them, once and for all: 'When I became an adult, I put an end to childish ways.'

For our encouragement, however, since none of us has achieved a 100 per cent record in liberating ourselves from childishness in thought, word or deed, we need to be assured that Paul wasn't claiming that his own love was now so perfect that he was free from such things. Again, we must remember that his words should be understood in the context of the end time and age to come. The fullness of spiritual maturity will not be realized until the day when God draws all things and all people to himself. Of course, that is no excuse for us adults who may still, on occasion, find ourselves lapsing into childish attitudes and behaviour. But it is an enormous relief to know that although we haven't yet arrived at perfect love, we are, by the grace of God, getting there, and one day will arrive at our destination!

We have Paul to thank for such encouragement. As an apostle of the Church of Jesus Christ, a major part of his task was helping people towards their full maturity in Christ, and he knew it wouldn't be fully realized in this life. This is how he puts it: 'It is he whom we proclaim, warning everyone and teaching everyone in all wisdom, so that we may present everyone mature in Christ. For this I toil and struggle with all the energy that he powerfully inspires within me' (Colossians 1.28–29). He knew from his own experience that it takes a lifetime and more to reach full spiritual maturity, for even as he neared the end of his amazingly effective ministry he admitted that he still had a way to go before he reached the final goal (Philippians 3.12–15).

So it is with us. It takes a lifetime and more before immaturity is finally put behind us, and every impediment to fullness of maturity within the love of God is removed. When that day dawns, the child, and the adult, will have grown to full stature in Christ.

Essential image

But, if it doesn't sound too Irish, in leaving behind our childhood, we must hold on to, and never forget, the essential image of the child, because without it we may struggle to reach our full stature in Christ. Let me explain.

When Paul uses the personal illustration of human experience and says, 'When I was a child, I spoke like a child, I thought like a child, I reasoned like a child; when I became an adult, I put an end to childish ways', he is reinforcing a vital point he has already made. He wants them to be in no doubt of the temporary nature of spiritual gifts. They would pass away with this present age, just as childhood passes away with the coming of adulthood. The love that forms the great theme of his song, however, belonged to a different category; it would never come to an end.

But in the meantime the image of the child has much to offer us as we journey along the road to spiritual maturity. It is not without significance that it was Jesus, in whom the love of God was perfected, who also used an illustration of the child to get this point across. When his disciples asked, 'Who is the greatest in the kingdom of heaven?', Jesus shocked them with his response. 'He called a child, whom he put among them, and said, "Truly I tell you, unless you change and become like children, you will never enter the kingdom of heaven. Whoever becomes humble like this child is the greatest in the kingdom of heaven. Whoever welcomes one such child in my name welcomes me"' (Matthew 18.2–5). In a society where not much importance was attached to children until they reached the age of puberty, this was a dramatic lesson for the disciples, just as Paul's song about the necessity and supremacy of love would have been to the Christians in Corinth.

Its implications are clear: children are not self-sufficient; they are utterly dependent, vulnerable and weak. They are trusting, ready to be helped and enlightened. They are eager, sometimes too eager, to grow up, and determined to make progress. They are keen to love, and perhaps most important of all they are ready to be loved. 'To such as these', Jesus reminded us, 'the kingdom of God belongs. Truly I tell you, whoever does not receive the kingdom of God as a little child will never enter it' (Mark 10.14–15).

Growing up

There is all the difference in the world between being childish and being childlike. We must put an end to childish ways if we are to become mature adults. We must become childlike if we are to enter the kingdom, and in our proper growth toward full spiritual maturity we must think, speak and reason as adults, without forgetting the child's readiness to love and be loved.

10

Face to face

For now we see in a mirror dimly,
but then we will see face to face.
Now I know only in part;
then I will know fully,
even as I have been fully known.

As a special treat, my wife Anne and I took our Sunday school class to the seaside for a day's outing. The children, all from a deprived inner-city area, were very excited and predictably had eaten their picnic lunches on the train, long before elevenses. It meant, of course, that immediately on arrival they went straight to the beach for a swim and a variety of games on the sand. As the morning wore on, the clouds gathered and it began to rain. It didn't dampen their enthusiasm, however, for on the way from the station they had spotted a huge indoor funfair, and in a moment of weakness we agreed to take them there.

I'm glad we did, for we relived part of our childhood. It was years since we had ridden on the dodgems, licked candyfloss and eaten toffee apples. With such delights on offer, the afternoon passed quickly and we started to round them up, ready for the return journey, only to discover that half of them were missing. Fortunately, before panic set in, we heard and recognized screams of laughter coming from one end of the concourse. Several of them had found the hall of mirrors, and were pulling faces and gyrating wildly in front of them. Fantastic images were produced, tubby children became thin, skinny ones became fat, homely ones became beautiful and handsome ones became ugly – all with the help of mirrors. We eventually enticed them away in time to have fish and chips before boarding the train. On the way home, tired as they were, they did little else but talk and laugh about the fun they had in the hall of mirrors.

Local industry

Members of Paul's congregation in Corinth probably didn't laugh at his reference to mirrors, though they may have listened more intently, for the manufacture of mirrors was a local industry and may even have provided employment for one or two of those present. Corinth was famous for its mirrors which, like most of those produced in the first century, were made of highly polished metal. Though, no doubt, there were different quality products on offer, they all had their shortcomings and, since Christians tended to be among the poorer sections of the community, perhaps Paul was describing mirrors that weren't exactly 'top of the range'.

But, whatever the quality, the reflection would not be very clear, and various words are used to describe this imperfection, for instance, 'dimly' (NRVS), 'puzzling reflections' (REB), 'poor reflection' (NIV), 'darkly' (AV). Behind all these descriptions is a common theme, namely, indistinctiveness. It wasn't always possible to make out exactly what you were looking at in the Corinthian mirrors. They were certainly more reliable than those experienced by our Sunday school children but nevertheless 'rather dim and somewhat distorted' would probably be a fair description of the quality of their reflection.

This view is reinforced by the basic meaning of the original word translated 'dimly'. The Jerusalem Bible translation gives us the clue when it speaks of the reflections in the mirror as 'mere riddles'. The word comes from the same source as our word 'enigmatic'. In other words, the reflection from the metal mirrors was obscure and indistinct.

The message thus conveyed by Paul's figure of speech was unmistakable, especially to those who were inordinately proud of their special knowledge of the mysteries of God. Such knowledge was not only partial; it was also, by the nature of things, dim and shadowy. The reality was hidden, still to be revealed in the age to come. It is true, we can and do see God in this world. We catch glimpses of his handiwork in nature and his footsteps in history. We see him in people and in the Scriptures. Supremely, we see him in Jesus Christ, who is the perfect image of God, but even then we are only able to grasp a part of the truth revealed. This shouldn't surprise us. The first disciples, who lived and worked closely with him, were at times puzzled and bewildered by what he said and did. They didn't always understand him, and at times their assessment of his person and work was totally wrong. After the resurrection and with the help of the Holy Spirit, they gradually came to a greater understanding, and began to rewrite their lives. Even at that point, however, a spiritual giant like Paul included himself in the description 'we see in a mirror, dimly'. It was an admission that his knowledge of God was still only partial. As yet, his sight was limited, as it were, by imperfect reflections, as in a mirror.

It is a salutary reminder that however advanced we might be in our knowledge of God, however experienced we might be in the work of God and however mature we may have become in the ways of God, we are still in need of greater clarity and enlightenment. We have seen only an indistinct and shadowy reflection, as in a first-century mirror. This fact should help dispel any foolish pride we may have in the extent of our knowledge of God. Hopefully, it should also increase our excitement and expectancy at the prospect of the shadow giving way to substance and the reflection being replaced by reality.

Face to face

Of course, reality isn't always what it is made out to be these days. We live in a computerized society, where with the right technology and the push of a button we can enter and interact with the world of virtual reality, not unlike that experienced by Alice in *Through the Looking Glass*. Yet even that so-called reality, in which our children have become experts, is bound by the limits of our sight. We continue to see through a mirror dimly, until such time as virtual reality is replaced by ultimate reality, on the day when we come into the unimpeded presence and glory of the God who is love.

'Face to face' is how Paul describes it. On his lips, however, this familiar expression is much more than a mere figure of speech. It touches on a theme of great importance in Paul's proclamation of the gospel, a point he underlines when he tells us that the Holy Spirit is the guarantee that this 'face-to-face knowing' will take place (2 Corinthians 1.22; 5.5). It clearly is a vital part of God's purpose for his people in the age to come, when he will draw all things to himself, including us! Paul gave us a foretaste of what that might mean in some other words he wrote to the Corinthians: 'For it is the God who said, "Let light shine out of darkness", who has shone in our hearts to give the light of the knowledge of the glory of God in the face of Jesus Christ' (2 Corinthians 4.6).

There is an intimate connection between the glory of God and the face of Jesus Christ. Indeed, Paul tells us that the glory of God is focused in the face of Christ. He goes even further by reminding us that the glory of God is shared with us through the ministry of the Holy Spirit (2 Corinthians 3.18), through whom God's eternal purpose is being achieved, as we are 'conformed to the image of his Son' (Romans 8.29).

That is a truly staggering thought, the implications of which have a direct bearing on the phrase 'face to face'. It means that in this present life, with the help of the Holy Spirit, who takes and shows us those things that belong to Christ (John 16.15), we can see, and begin to experience, something of the glory of God in the face of Jesus Christ as we are transformed into his likeness or image. In other words, we anticipate in this life, however partially, the conformity to Christ that we shall experience perfectly in the life to come.

At this point, humility demands that we remind ourselves again that we still only 'see in a mirror, dimly'. We don't yet know the full extent of what that face-to-face meeting will mean. But certain things have been revealed. John, in his first letter, acknowledges this uncertainty and assurance when he writes, 'Beloved, we are God's children now; what we will be has not yet been revealed. What we do know is this: when he is revealed, we will be like him, for we will see him as he is' (1 John 3.2). There is a proper ignorance for Christians to admit, and there is an appropriate assurance for Christians to maintain. The full knowledge of our redeemed life in heaven must wait until Christ appears and we arrive. But the one thing we do know is that the full knowledge of the glory of God will be seen in the face of Jesus Christ. He shall be revealed, we will see him face to face and, incredible though it may seem, we will be like him.

The mere thought of that, let alone the reality of it, is truly awesome, in the proper sense of that word, and brings to mind a little chorus I learned as a young Christian:

> Turn your eyes upon Jesus,
>   Look full in his wonderful face
> And the things of earth will grow strangely dim
>   In the light of his glory and grace.

Though it is true that, in the light of the knowledge of the glory of God in the face of Jesus Christ, the partial things of earth may fade into insignificance, it is worth noting John's words immediately following his remarkable statement about seeing Christ and being like him. 'All who have this hope', he says, 'purify themselves, just as he is pure' (1 John 3.3). He was convinced that our vision of heaven, and our face-to-face meeting with Christ, must not be detached from our Christian experience and responsibility here on earth. They are intimately and vitally connected.

Now and then

This linking of heavenly vision and earthly responsibility was also a central feature of Paul's writings, including his song of love. Time and time again in his letters, he would expound and proclaim the glorious vision of what the grace of God in Christ had done and would do. As often as not, this was followed by the word 'therefore', which would mark the beginning of practical advice regarding the everyday responsibilities of life.

A classic example of this is found in his letter to the Ephesians. At the close of the first three chapters, containing superb insights and wonderful teaching about the grace of God and the power of the gospel, he ends with this marvellous prayer and doxology: 'Now to him who by the power at work within us is able to accomplish abundantly far more than all we can ask or imagine, to him be glory in the church and in Christ Jesus to all generations, for ever and ever. Amen' (Ephesians 3.20–21). In the light of such a magnificent vision of God's power and glory, we might be tempted to say, 'That's terrific. God's got it sorted, therefore, let's leave it all to him.' Paul takes the opposite view. The glorious vision is an incentive to practical Christian living. 'I therefore', he says, 'beg you to lead a life worthy of the calling to which you have been called, with all humility and gentleness, with patience, bearing with one another in love' (Ephesians 4.1–2).

Though he doesn't use the word 'therefore' in his song of love, its implication is clearly visible. God is love. Therefore, since we and the whole of creation find our ultimate completeness in him, we are required to act in love throughout all the responsibilities and relationships of daily life. Love is supreme and never comes to an end, therefore all other things, like tongues, knowledge and prophecy, must be kept in proper perspective, so that the Church on earth can grow in unity and love.

But it is particularly in the repetition of the two words 'now' and 'then', that Paul links heaven and earth, and reminds us that each holds practical implications for the other. Because of the 'then', that is, the fullness of the knowledge of the glory of God in the face of Jesus Christ, and the promise that we shall see him and be like him, the 'now' must be treated with thoughtfulness and care. Since, under the creative ministry of the Holy Spirit, the 'now' is a preparation for the 'then', it must be entered into with a practical commitment to anticipate, however partially, those things into which, with the help of God's grace, we shall one day enter fully. Because of what we will be 'then', it matters how we live 'now'.

Knowing and known

It is interesting that Paul, having begun his song with references to 'tongues, prophecy and knowledge', has dropped two of them and now refers to knowledge only. He clearly wants to highlight knowledge. Once again, it is the partial nature of what we know of God 'now' that is contrasted with the fullness, or totality, of what we shall know 'then'. 'I will know fully, even as I have been fully known.' The words are sublime and their evocative power is overwhelming. Doubtless they will resonate to each of us in slightly different ways, but for my part I find help in two personal reflections, one humorous and the other more serious. Both have a bearing on knowing and being known.

The first comes as a result of broadcasting regularly on BBC radio for nearly 25 years. During all this time I have been engaged in a pastoral ministry that has taken me across the country and into contact with thousands of people who listen regularly to the radio. Invariably, wherever I have gone, someone has always approached me and said, 'Are you the Roy Williamson that I hear on Radio Two?' Embarrassed, I usually reply, 'I'm afraid so,' and begin to chuckle because I know what's coming next, and it usually does. 'Oh!', say my enquirers, unable to keep the surprise and, I fear, the disappointment out of their voice, 'You're not as tall as your voice,' or 'You don't look like the way you sound.' 'I'm sorry about that,' I reply, 'but it's the way God made me!' We then have a proper laugh together.

It is natural for people to put faces to names, to imagine what a person looks like by the sound of their voice, though it must often come as a surprise, pleasant or otherwise, when they come face to face with the person concerned. The face is a revelation. To some extent it is a history lesson, revealing something of our past life, and a mirror reflecting aspects of our life in the present. Those Radio Two listeners 'knew' me as a voice, but for better or for worse they discovered there was more to me than that, when they saw me face to face.

My second personal reflection concerns a question I was asked as a late teenager. It ultimately led to my conversion, and went like this, 'Do you know Jesus?' I understood exactly what the questioner meant and was totally honest in my reply. 'No,' I said. Of course, having been taught well in Sunday school, I knew quite a bit about Jesus, but that wasn't what the questioner had in mind. He wanted to know if I had a personal relationship with Jesus. To that there was only one answer. I had a modicum of knowledge in my head but as yet it hadn't reached my heart or affected my will. 'No' was the honest answer to the question.

If I was asked that same question today, however, having shared a personal relationship with Jesus for over 50 years, the answer would be different, but just as honest: 'Yes, with qualifications.' There is so much about Jesus that I still don't know, so much that remains hidden, until all is revealed in that face-to-face meeting.

On that day, unlike those radio listeners, there will be neither surprise nor disappointment on the part of Jesus, for his knowledge of me is not partial, but already complete. In his love I am fully known and, amazingly, he still loves me! Unlike my love for him, which is weak and poor, his love for me remains constant and strong. It never comes to an end.

Also, in that same love, I will fully know. Unlike the dim reflection of the mirror, the vision will be clear and bright. The full and unimpeded sight of perfect love will almost certainly overwhelm me with a sense of awe and wonder, and fill me with praise to God for his mercy. How I will bear it, I know not, but the God who is love will fully enlighten me with the knowledge of his glory in the face of Jesus Christ.

I will know fully, even as I have been fully known.

11

Love supreme

And now faith, hope and love abide,
these three;
and the greatest of these is love.

Desert Island Discs is for many people, including me,
one of the highlights of the weekly programmes offered
by the BBC on Radio Four. The presenter is superb. The
variety of guests is wide. The stories they have to tell of
their life and work are truly fascinating and frequently
inspiring. The records they choose are always interesting,
though their taste in music is often an acquired one and,
depending on the predilections of the listener, can vary
from the sublime to the ridiculous.

The point of greatest interest for me, however, is reached
when towards the end of the programme the guests are
asked to choose one thing, in addition to the Bible and
Shakespeare, they would like to take with them onto the
desert island. Some choose 'fun things' to help them cope
with boredom or loneliness. Others choose practical things
that may help them survive, or even escape. Many choose
basic things, like toothpaste and toothbrush, or paper and
pencil. One recent guest asked for a solar-powered

computer, with a secret drawer containing cyanide, lest life became so intolerable he might wish to end it quickly. Most, however, choose something they couldn't imagine themselves living without – even on a desert island.

Essentials

There are times when all of us are forced by circumstances to reflect on those things that we couldn't live without. To begin with the list may be a lengthy one, especially if we take too much notice of television commercials and their pervasive insistence as to what constitutes the good life. As time progresses, however, and common sense prevails, the list becomes much shorter and more realistic. Things we once considered necessary are set aside as of no account. People are seen to be more important than things, relationships more valuable than possessions. The true essentials of life come into sharper focus and perhaps can be listed on the back of an envelope, if not a postage stamp, rather than in a large notebook.

When Paul reflected on the things he couldn't live without, he summed them up in three words: faith, hope and love. They formed a significant combination and provided a memorable conclusion to his song of love. They also describe the essentials for every life that claims to be Christian. That is one of the reasons, I believe, why Paul, somewhat surprisingly, includes all three in the final stanza of his song. In the light of all he had been saying in the previous verses, the use of the word love on its own, together with a ringing endorsement of its supremacy, would have made a suitable conclusion to his argument and a grand finale to his song. But he had another purpose in mind.

This beautiful trio of words occupies an important place in Paul's Christian witness. They occur repeatedly in his letters – part of a repertoire, it seems, upon which he drew frequently in order to remind the church of those things that were essential to its life. So, for instance, he encourages the Thessalonian Christians with these words: 'We always give thanks to God for all of you and mention you in our prayers, constantly remembering before our God and Father your work of faith and labour of love and steadfastness of hope in our Lord Jesus Christ' (1 Thessalonians 1.2–3). He does the same for the Christians in Colossae: 'We have heard of your faith in Christ Jesus and of the love that you have for all the saints, because of the hope laid up for you in heaven' (Colossians 1.4–5).

Here, at the end of his song of love in 1 Corinthians, he links them again in what is generally agreed to be the clearest and most striking combination of the three things that were so vital to him, and so essential to the life of the Christian Church: 'And now faith, hope and love abide, these three; and the greatest of these is love.'

'These three' are so significant because they represent the essence of the saving relationship between God and human beings. New life in Christ depends upon them. They describe our response to the grace of God in Christ. My Christian life began on the day when I consciously put my trust in God, in response to his love revealed through Christ on the cross. That same love, poured into my heart through the Holy Spirit, who is the first instalment of what God has promised, has filled me with a sure and certain hope of that which is to come, namely the kingdom of God in all its fullness. Faith, hope and love are essential to my Christian being and to my relationship with God.

There is also a sense of unity between the three and a feeling of eternity about them. Unlike the spiritual gifts mentioned earlier, which though valuable are temporary, these three abide, or remain. The Revised English Version refers to them as 'three things that last for ever'. Some feel, perhaps rightly, that in the full vision and glorious radiance of the God who is love faith and hope will become superfluous. Such a view is poetically expressed by John Stainer in his well-known words:

> Faith will vanish into sight,
> Hope be emptied in delight;
> Love in heaven will shine more bright...

That, however, doesn't seem to be what Paul is saying in the closing words of his song, as he prepares us for God's future. Indeed, he seems to be presenting faith, hope and love, as permanent, in contrast to the transient nature of the spiritual gifts he has mentioned earlier. Having been instrumental in fostering our new life in Christ, faith, hope and love will continue to be part of that new order of life that will be experienced in the kingdom of God.

Faith

How that faith will express itself in the immediate presence of God will undoubtedly be one of the many surprises that await us in glory. But having played such a key role in our Christian life on earth, it is hard to imagine life without it in the future which God has prepared for his people. It is worth noting that Paul, at this point, is not referring to the miracle-working faith that can remove mountains, mentioned at the beginning of his song (13.2). He is not speaking about spectacular things that God might do for us or through us, but about basic trust, a loving and grateful acceptance of God as he is, faithful and trustworthy.

Paul was the great exponent of such faith. It dominated his life and enabled him to say, 'The life I now live in the flesh I live by faith in the Son of God, who loved me and gave himself for me' (Galatians 2.20). It was fundamental not only to his life but also to his teaching, and his letters are full of it. It is impossible to overestimate the influence that Paul's teaching on faith has had in the Church across the Christian centuries. His message was consistent, profound and clear. God is faithful. The God who made himself known in Jesus can be trusted for everything – past, present and future. We can take him at his word. What he has promised, he will fulfil.

Faith in Jesus Christ makes God accessible to us through his Holy Spirit. However weak it may be, faith is a sign of our relationship with God, and we must not restrict it to this life only. If the essence of faith is trust in God and commitment to him, it is unlikely to be made redundant in the coming age. If the dim reflection of God, as in a mirror, inspires our faith and commitment in this life, how much greater will be our response of gratitude and trust when we see him face to face, in the life to come?

'We love God because he first loved us,' wrote John (1 John 4.19). That is, we came to trust and love God because of God's initiative. Faith responded to love. Surely, therefore, faith will continue to flower in the presence of the God who is love.

Hope

If faith continues to flourish in the age to come, so also will hope, for they are closely related. Hope is faith focused on the future.

Though hope may have its eyes mainly on the future, it is a very practical and necessary part of our present life and experience. We cannot live without hope. To a large extent, this is true of all people and not just those who have faith in Christ. Two of the great social justice movements of our time, for instance, were the result of the nurturing of hope, against all the odds, in the hearts of men and women. The anti-apartheid movement in South Africa and the civil rights movement in the USA found their energy and inspiration in the hope that goodness would triumph over evil. The conviction that all people were created equal in the sight of God inspired leaders like Nelson Mandela and Dr Martin Luther King to negate the negative attitudes surrounding them and to see that hope fulfilled in their lifetime.

This is the essence of Christian hope. It is a confident hope, based not on a smiling optimism but on the resurrection of Jesus, and the experience of the Spirit already given, in which some aspects of God's future are brought right into the present moment. It was this creative and anticipatory work of the Spirit that enabled Paul to see, even in the sufferings and frustrations of the world, signs of hope. The tribulations of the world were part of the birth pangs of the new life and liberty that is God's purpose for the whole of creation (Romans 8.18–25).

By combining hope with faith and love as things which abide, or last for ever, Paul is implying that though hope will be realized in the age to come it will not disappear or be set aside. Hope is eternally linked with God. It is part of the unchangeable truth about God, as Paul emphasizes in his prayer for the Christians in Rome: 'May the God of hope fill you with all joy and peace in believing, so that you may abound in hope by the power of the Holy Spirit' (Romans 15.13).

When in the age to come we dwell in the presence of the God of hope, and of the Spirit who helps us abound in hope, it is hard to imagine that the God who has given us such hope will cease to inspire and maintain it, or that we will cease to express and enjoy it. Heaven might be a rather dull place if that were the case. But since boredom has no place in the character of God, monotony is unlikely to be on the agenda in heaven.

Quite early in my Christian discipleship I made a point of reading the whole of the Bible in depth and slowly discovering what the key words and themes were all about. I have never forgotten the definition of hope that I learned in those days, namely, 'the well-founded expectation of coming good'. It isn't slick, but it is biblical. Our hope is certainly well-founded in the cross and resurrection of Jesus, the anticipatory presence and work of the Holy Spirit as a guarantee of what is to come and, supremely, in the character of God the Father. If I may put it like this, on the day when we see 'face to face', hope's expectation will come to fruition, but that will not be the end of the matter. As long as God lives, and we dwell in his presence, hope will continue. There will always be a well-founded expectation of good to come. It could not be otherwise, for God is love and his love is eternal.

Love

So Paul concludes his song by returning to his central theme of love. While retaining the word *agape* for love there is, throughout his song, a gentle shift of meaning from one section to another. As he speaks of the ineffectiveness of spiritual gifts without love, he is referring to our love for one another (13.1–3). When he describes the basic nature of love (13.4–7), his model is clearly Jesus Christ, for only he could measure up to such perfect love. As he begins, in the final section (13.8–13), to speak of the enduring quality and permanence of love, it is manifestly the love of God, to be revealed in its fullness at the end of the age, that he has in mind. We need to note, however, that that is the love personified in Jesus and reflected in our love for one another. Divine love has been the fundamental theme throughout his song, for all love has its source in God. Love is as permanent as God, for God is love.

Therein, I believe, lies the reason why love is declared to be the greatest. It is the essential nature of God. God doesn't trust and he doesn't hope, but he can't stop loving without being untrue to his nature. His love is always outgoing, always unconditional.

It was so from the beginning of time. The world in which we live is the creation of God's love. Creation was not simply a demonstration of God's boundless power, but a communication of his blazing, unconditional love, and it will be so at the end of time when his kingdom comes in all its fullness. His eternal love will embrace and enfold us, and restore his perfect image in us. This was made possible by what the God of love did between the beginning and the end of time.

The cross and resurrection are not specifically mentioned in Paul's song of love, but they underwrite every aspect of it, for they take us into the heart of the love of God. 'God so loved the world that he gave his only Son.' The resurrection of Jesus was God's approval of his self-giving life and death. Self-giving is at the heart of all love because it is at the heart of the God of love. So, although we must in faith, hope and love wait in joyful expectation of the full revelation of the knowledge of glory of God in the face of Jesus Christ, we must never forget that the cross is the place of God's decisive self-disclosure. It was there that the power and the glory associated with God's own being was revealed as the saving power of redeeming love. Thanks be to God!

Epilogue

The personal reflections contained in this little book make no pretence at being a scholarly exposition of one of the great chapters of the Bible. I hesitated long and hard before daring to write about such a sublime song of love, lest my treatment of it would demean its beauty, or even worse produce boredom rather than interest for my readers. In the end, I couldn't, with integrity, escape the challenge. For years the words of the song have tripped all too easily off my tongue, but just how deeply they have penetrated my heart or radically affected the way I live is a moot point – and one which I could not ignore.

'All you need is love', sang the Beatles, but did they mean the self-giving love that is the essence of God's nature and disclosed so dramatically at the cross? I don't know. But I have discovered, and in this small volume tried to explain, a little of what St Paul meant when he spoke of love, and it has thrilled my soul. At the same time, it has prompted serious self-examination regarding the words I speak, the attitudes I adopt, the value I place upon people and things and, above all, upon the vision I hold of God and his kingdom.

Love is a gift, a fruit of the Spirit. It is not something dragged up with a massive self-effort from the hidden depths of our being. It is not something that is speedily and superficially applied on the surface to meet public demand or expectation. It is a gift of God; it comes from the generous heart of God himself.

Love is also a demand, not in the sense of a tyrant standing over us with a big stick, but in the form of a lover drawing out from us a response of love that will transfigure our lives and prepare us for life in God's unimaginably wonderful future. Love is the language of the kingdom of God. While on earth we will not be able to measure up fully to the demands of love as outlined in Paul's song. Time and again we may fall short, repent, find forgiveness, and start again. For our encouragement, however, when love controls our words and deeds, inspires our thoughts and motivates our actions, God's future has come into the present. God teaches us to love here, among all the complexities and frustrations of life on earth, in order that we might begin to learn the language of heaven.

References

Mission Praise, Marshall Pickering, 1990
New English Hymnal, Canterbury Press, 1986
Stott, J. R. W., *The Epistles of John*, Tyndale Press, 1964
Ward, Hannah, and Jennifer Wild (eds), *Christian Quotation Collection*, Lion, 1997

Further reading

Barclay, William, *The Letters to the Corinthians*, Saint Andrew Press, 1975

Barrett, C. K., *The First Epistle to the Corinthians*, A. & C. Black, 1988

Bruce, F. F., 1 and 2 Corinthians, *Oliphants*, 1971

Dunn, James D. G., *Jesus and the Spirit*, SCM Press, 1975

Furnish, V. P., *The Theology of the First Letter to the Corinthians*, Cambridge University Press, 1999

Godet, F., *Commentary on Corinthians I*, Vol 2, Kregel Publications, 1982

Grosheide, F. W., *The First Epistle to the Corinthians*, Marshall, Morgan & Scott, 1953

Morris, Leon, *1 Corinthians*, Inter-Varsity Press, 1985

Murphy-O'Connor, Jerome, *1 Corinthians*, Bible Reading Fellowship, 1997

Young, Frances, and David F. Ford, *Meaning and Truth in 2 Corinthians*, SPCK, 1987

Wright, Tom, *Paul for Everyone: 1 Corinthians*, SPCK, 2003